AR Lewis

RYA Advanced Windsurfing

Words by Simon Bornhoft
Edited by Amanda Van Santen

CW005553667

© RYA 2010
First Published 2010
The Royal Yachting Association
RYA House, Ensign Way, Hamble
Southampton SO31 4YA
Tel: 0844 556 9555
Fax: 0844 556 9516
Email: publications@rya.org.uk
Web: www.rya.org.uk
ISBN: 978-1-905104598
RYA Order Code: G52

Totally Chlorine
Free

Sustainable
Forests

A CIP record of this book is available from the British Library

Note: While all reasonable care has been taken in the preparation of this book, the publisher takes no responsibility for the use of the methods or products or contracts described in the book.

Telephone 0844 556 9555 for a free copy of our Publications Catalogue.

Cover Design: Pete Galvin
Photographs: Karen Bornhoft
Illustrations: Pete Galvin
Typeset: Creativebyte
Proofreading and indexing: Alan Thatcher
Printed in China through: World Print
Acknowledgments: Minorca Sailing Holidays, Chichester Watersports Centre, Simon Winkley, Gul, Mark Warner

Contents

RYA Advanced Windsurfing

Advanced Windsurfing is a companion sequel to RYA Start Windsurfing (G49) and RYA Intermediate Windsurfing (G51). It is designed for windsurfers who already have good basic knowledge of the sport and are looking to reach a higher level. The book will show you how to windsurf in higher winds, overcoming problems that halt your progress, while mastering key transitions such a faster tacks, gybes and more advanced moves.

The fundamental skills of windsurfing, covered by RYA Start Windsurfing and RYA Intermediate Windsurfing, work right through the sport. Your progression to advanced level windsurfing is all about applying basic principles of the sport to more demanding environments.

Finding the confidence to accomplish new moves often relies on greater commitment to basic windsurfing principles. For instance, the actions of getting into the straps on a sub-100 litre board are pretty much identical to getting into the straps on a much larger 180 litre board. It just requires a little more precision and a lot more commitment!

All of the RYA Windsurfing Handbooks are designed to enhance your current knowledge and use key principles to raise your level. RYA Advanced Windsurfing repeats the Fastfwd Formula, demonstrating key transition skills and how they become even more important in advanced areas of the sport. Additional tips and coaching exercises will help take you through to the next level.

Smaller boards and stronger winds often create barriers that may seem impossible to overcome. Follow the guidelines and skills' training exercises set out in RYA Advanced Windsurfing, and you will be able to develop the confidence, skills and consistency required for the next windsurfing level.

Whether you're seeking to crack waterstarts, drop a few litres in board volume, improve your overall blasting ability, make fluid tacks, gybes or move into freestyle – we're with you all the way!

RYA Advanced Windsurfing Course

When you have completed an RYA Advanced Windsurfing Course or specific clinics, the instructor will log your progression in the RYA National Windsurfing Logbook and Syllabus (G47). The Centre principal or chief instructor will decide whether a certificate is to be awarded, or advise you that further practice is required, providing a clear pathway to your certificate.

Creating a Learning Environment

People often struggle, take years or even fail to master techniques because they don't approach learning in a positive strategic way. Here are some key factors that have little to do with windsurfing ability, but can contribute hugely towards your success. The most important factor here is to make these points part of your game plan.

Correct location & conditions

- It sounds obvious, but make sure the conditions and your equipment are right for what you're trying to do. Sailing under or overpowered or on too large or too small a board immediately restricts your prospects. (See board volume selection chart page 90)

- Choose a suitable location for what you're trying to learn. Seek gently shelving water for waterstarts. Find safe, shallow, flat water to reduce fatigue and experiment with new moves and encourage skills training.

- Once you've mastered waterstarts, look to progress on safe, shallow, coastal locations that provide strong clear winds, with the least possible tide, especially when venturing onto sub-100L boards.

Be specific

- Blasting up and down might be fun, but it is a long road to success. Be more focused and specific about what you're trying to learn and be prepared to break away from hacking up and down all day.

- Multi tasking is not easy at speed. Try to identify and accentuate one key point at a time. For example, don't just throw yourself into fast tacks. Say to yourself, "On this tack, no matter what happens, I'll accentuate on my vision and make it a priority to look out of the turn." Or, "No matter what else happens, I'll wrap my foot round that mast base and oppose that rig." This is why we've broken moves like gybing into three specific parts and isolated the beginning and ends of moves, and suggesting how to practise them in isolation.

Honest feedback

- You might think or feel those knees were bent mid gybe, but actually you were standing to attention. So get decent feedback, get coached, watch yourself on video and be really honest with yourself.

Lighter winds & dry land

It's easy to become a wind junkie and turn the car around unless the trees are doubled over or you can't use your favourite small sail, but this approach seriously reduces your chances of progress. For example, if you try 30 gybes in a windy session and spend 1-2 seconds changing your feet mid-gybe, you might only be spending ONE MINUTE in total trying to master a major or vital aspect of the gybe in a whole day. Get out and practise in light winds! Simulating body, hand, foot and rig actions on land and in light to marginal winds also offers a fabulous opportunity to isolate key skills and repeat them in a 'controlled' situation. So whilst the lure of planing windsurfing is very appealing, remember to use lighter winds to practise the finer details.

Coach's Corner

Make the most of every practice session

- Accentuate your actions!

- Don't underestimate the basics.

- If things 'go wrong' look at what you were doing before the problems started.

- If it's a constant struggle, stop and refocus on what's needed to rectify a problem.

- Always enjoy your windsurfing. Everything is possible with the right attitude, strategy and technique.

Fastfwd Formula

To help make your progression as quick and easy as possible, the RYA and Simon Bornhoft have created the Fastfwd Formula. If you haven't heard or seen the Fastfwd Formula before, then you're about to discover the five defining principles and supportive skills that are essential to the sport at every level. Whilst you might, on occasions, heavily accentuate one particular element, they all come together to support your actions on a board.

It is easy to say, "Okay these are the basics, what about the advanced stuff?" Well it's right here! Without these five skills it is impossible to successfully add the finer details of the more advanced clinics. Working towards your objectives or problem solving comes straight back to following and exaggerating the main mantras in the Formula.

Here's a short summary of what the elements represent:

VISION to maintain your sailing line – 'Look where you want to go.'

TRIM to keep the board flat – 'Create a stable platform for everything you do.'

BALANCE to form your framework – 'Always oppose the rig's forces, position and movement.'

POWER to channel the rig's forces – 'Sheet the boom in, back and down.'

STANCE – How we use our body, demonstrated by Straight 7 and Super 7 extremes:

Straight 7 for acceleration – 'Lift and lock the hips, tighten the torso & push through toes.'

Super 7 for controlling acceleration – 'Drop the hips and dig or weight the heels.'

You'll see how the whole Formula forms the basis of virtually everything you'll do on ANY board, including Getting Going, Steering, Early Planing, Harnessing, Footstraps and Blasting Control.

Transitional skills

When it comes to transitions, the five main elements are an integral part of your success. Two specific transitional skills will help complete moves like tacks and gybes.

- Shifting & Switching – A very specific movement of the hips and feet mid-tack or mid-gybe.

- Rig Rotator – A specific action to 'rotate' the rig in non-planing & planing gybes. Also used in Helicopter Tacks, Push Tacks, Cowboys, Sail 360's and Spocks.

VISION helps maintain your sailing line on the board…

Look in the direction of where you want to go. This simple rule tops all the other elements in the Formula. Looking forward, through and out of turns, rather than down or at the equipment, has an incredible effect on your balance and ability to control direction of travel, plus it makes your actions more dynamic and fluid. This is particularly relevant when making fast tacks, all styles of gybes and just about every other advanced move.

Getting Vision sorted is massively important for advanced windsurfing.

Top Tips

- So simple – 'Look where you want to go!'
- Look forward – for early planing, harnessing, getting into footstraps, improving your stance, reading the wind and water state, as well as changes in your sailing line.
- Look downwind – to sail or turn downwind, when you increase speed or look through a gybe.
- Look upwind – to sail or turn upwind when controlling excess speed or preparing for a tack.

Techniques that require Vision are not only advantageous for blasting control and steering, but they also play a key role in transitions.

Coach's Corner

Get it right

- Make sure you are on the right sailing line for what you are trying to achieve. Focus on looking forward and planning ahead.

- Then try a few runs, fast tacks, gybes or other moves. Focus hard on looking forward, where you want to go and where you want to end up facing.

Gybing
Look into and out of the gybe to improve rig control, release awareness and lead you through the gybe.

Tacking
Look upwind on entry and especially on to guarantee tidy, well executed tacks.

Helicopter tack
Look out of the turn to pull through advanced moves like the helicopter tack.

Don't lose your head!
Make sure you don't look down or watch the rig during tacks and gybes. This will greatly reduce your stability, increasing the chance of going into the water with the rig!

Trim the Board Flat

The smaller the board, the less stable it will be and the more sensitive it becomes to foot pressure, body positioning and rig movement. So there needs to be even greater determination to keep the board flat on the water. Excessive sideways tilt, sudden sinking of the nose or too much weight on the tail instantly cause control problems.

You can't just stand on top of the board and ride along. Due to higher speeds, forces through your legs and feet play a huge role in control over the board's trim.

Feet forward to hold the board flat and make it plane.

Trim out of the footstraps

- Front foot points forward to drive the board flat and forwards.
- Rear foot goes across the board to control sideways tilt.

Trim at slower speeds

Move forward and inboard, with increased toe pressure.

Bringing both feet well forward and pushing through your toes prevents the tail from dragging and helps acceleration. You often need to be standing further forward than you think, even forward of the front straps to promote very early planing.

Trim in the footstraps

As a general guide, try to keep equal weight on both legs. The only time this alters is when turning or heading downwind or upwind, which requires increased pressure through rear and front leg. However, what really matters when you are in the straps at speed is the transfer of weight between your heels and toes.

Trim at higher speeds

Move your feet back and outboard, with increased heel pressure. This provides much greater control and resistance as the board accelerates, plus your feet are well positioned to get into the straps.

Trim to encourage acceleration

Pushing through the toes is particularly relevant in a marginal wind just after getting into the harness and footstraps, at which point you should be in a Straight 7 stance. It is also really effective when heading downwind in the lead up to a gybe, when you should adopt a Super 7 Drop & Push stance.

Trim to control acceleration

Dig and weight the heels, pulling up on your toes to lock the windward rail down. This is especially important on the front foot.

Trimming with your back leg

Try bending your back leg to see what a massive role it plays in altering trim. If you are sailing in marginal winds, bending the rear knee will help to reduce tail sink. If you are sailing at speed in choppy, bouncy conditions, try heavily flexing the back leg. This will limit nose lift and, settle the board and avoid spin-out.

Sinking, slowing & stumbling

It's very common to over straighten the back leg and overweight the back foot. This alone can cause the tail to sink, prevent acceleration and seriously reduce control. A quick flex of the rear knee can normally get you out of trouble.

Wrong! The tail sinks and you lose control.

Balance Frames your Windsurfing

At higher speeds and in more challenging situations, the need to be balanced and in control of the rig at all stages is paramount. An advanced sailor must constantly work to oppose the rig's position and counter-balance the forces and movement of the rig. Two main factors create counter-balance.

1. Keep your distance from the rig by extending the front arm.

2. Always oppose the force and movement of the body to create a counter-balance. Essentially this means that if ever the body moves one way, the mast/rig should be moved in the opposite direction.

Making the movement

Sometimes the counter-balancing movement can be minimal, at other times it needs to be hugely exaggerated. The movement is applicable to non-planing and blasting, as well as steering, tacks, beachstarts, waterstarts, gybes, wave riding and 99% of all freestyle moves.

Coach's Corner

Gybing counter-balance

Your counter-balancing skills will be tested to their limit when gybing! The crucial stage is mid-gybe when changing your foot position and rotating the rig. Note how the body is leaning into the turn and the rig is leaning out of the turn. Classic opposition!

Tacking counter-balance

Virtually every move works by opposing the movement of the body with the rig. None more so than in the middle of a tack, when you should force the rig to leeward as your body shifts to windward. A common error is to pull the rig too close to your body, which consequently sinks the nose and you fall in backwards.

Coach's Corner

Full opposition

If you look at any intermediate or advanced freestyle tricks, opposing the rig's movement with your body is the catalyst for the move that allows all the nuances and finer details to actually work.

Out of opposition

When things go wrong, nine times out of ten it is due to lack of counter-balance. This could be pulling the mast too close to the body, leaning or falling the same way as the rig.

Use Power to Channel Rig Forces

Power is achieved by the simple action of sheeting in: pulling the boom in, back and down. However, in stronger winds and at higher speeds, POWER needs to be really accentuated. It is such a major factor in improving TRIM and maintaining control of the rig when getting going, blasting in the straps and setting up for moves. Don't underestimate how much you can and should commit to the rig when fully sheeting the boom. Not just in towards the centreline and back towards the tail, but also down through the harness lines.

Out of the harness
When getting going or coming out of tacks and gybes, it's vital to sheet the boom in, back and down before getting into the harness and footstraps.

In the harness
Sinking down into the harness and pushing outboard through an extended front leg forms a brace to enable your rear hip, shoulder and back arm to move well outboard. This effectively sheets the clew in just over the leeward edge of the tail. In stronger winds, massively accentuate the POWER: use your entire body weight, and adopt a Super 7 Drop & Dig stance. Really sit back in your harness and hang down off the boom.

Coach's Corner

Exit from a gybe

In 'non-blasting' situations, when you want control and security, such as when exiting tacks, gybes or finishing moves like waterstarts, jumps and freestyle use the down aspect of POWER to increase your control over the rig and TRIM the board.

Why do you lose control?

If you often lose control, stop suddenly and have difficulty maintaining speed or directional stability, it is often down to sheeting out too much, or pulling the body too close to the boom. This is most likely to happen when blasting at speed or unhooking and setting up for gybes. To solve the problem, try the following:

Wrong! your body is too close to the boom.

1. When rigging, position the boom high enough so that the harness lines pull down on the boom.

2. On the water, make sure your front arm is extended and place both hands well down the boom to get more leverage over the sail.

3. Are the harness lines far enough back? There should be very little effort needed in the arms. If you are straining, try moving them.

Body Stance on a Board

We've shown how VISION, TRIM, BALANCE and POWER all play a key role in your success on a board. But the final piece of the jigsaw that massively affects your experience on a board will be STANCE, which detemines how you alter the alignment of your body and direct specific forces through the torso, hips, legs and feet. It's so important to realise that you are not aiming to ride on top of the board in a 'perfect' fixed position. You need to move, react, drive and gain command by regularly altering the alignment and commitment of the body's forces to drive, push and direct the board where you want it to go!

The basis of a perfect stance

- When in the harness, adopt a relaxed grip. You should be able to move your hands up and down the boom.

- With extended arms, adopt an overhand grip with the backhand and an overhand (especially for gybing) or underhand grip on the front hand.

- Avoid high elbows, heavily flexed arms and standing too upright. The aim is to form the shape of a number 7 with your body.

The secret of the number 7!
Note how the first four elements of the Formula help form the number 7 shape:
VISION – Look forward over front shoulder.
TRIM – Extend the front leg; the back leg flexes to suit different situations.
BALANCE – Extend the front arm to keep the shoulders outboard and oppose the rig.
POWER – The rear arm also moves outboard to help sheet the rig.

Exact styles will vary from person to person, but we all have to alter the alignment of our body to direct specific forces to suit changing conditions and situations. These are positive actions!

Straight 7 'Lift & Lock' to increase acceleration

Light/marginal wind stance.

When sailing along (in or out of the harness) and you feel power from the sail reduce, switch into a 'Straight 7' stance. This is particularly applicable just after hooking-in, getting in the straps, heading upwind or trying to keep planing through a lull.

1. Narrow your hand spread to inside shoulder width. Narrow your foot spread if out of the straps.

2. Adopt a very light grip rather than pulling heavily on your arms when hooked-in with the harness.

3. Fully extend the body and tighten the torso/stomach by lifting and locking the hips.

4. Push through the toes to help TRIM.

Strong wind and over powered stance.

Super 7 – Drop & Dig to control acceleration

The opposite end of the stance spectrum is the exaggerated Super 7 'Drop & Dig' action for stronger winds when you might feel like the board is lurching from 1st to 4th gear. It offers extra control while you get hooked in and strapped up.

1. Widen your hand spread to just past shoulder width. Widen foot spread if out of the straps.

2. Keep front leg extended to push hips well outboard.

3. Drop hips down by bending the back leg.

4. Dig heels to hold windward rail down. Pull up on toes, especially inside front strap.

5. Roll upper body slightly, pointing the elbows down to accentuate POWER and the 'drop and dig' action.

Super 7 Drop & Dig in the straps

In speedier and more dynamic situations you often need to adopt a fully committed Super 7 'Drop & Dig' stance. The hips drop down and out by pushing against the windward rail with equally weighted legs. This action helps sheet the sail in and encourages you to apply substantial pressure on the windward rail by digging the heels (especially the front foot) onto the edge of the board. Once in the straps, pull up on the toes (primarily the front foot) which adds that final touch to help maintain control. It is all to do with the movement of the hips and not pulling on the arms!

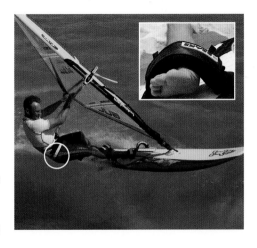

Getting going: Super 7 Drop & Push

In many windy situations we use a dynamic Super 7 stance, but rather than dig on the heels you push through the toes to drive the board forward. Typical uses include:

- Coming up on to the board after a beachstart or waterstart.
- Exiting a tack, when the rig is thrown forward.
- Setting-up for non-planing or planing gybes.
- Just before and after rotating the rig at the end of a gybe.
- Recovering tricky situations and exiting moves like Tacks, Jumps, Helicopter Tacks, Push Tacks and even Loops!

Top tip

Using body weight is far more effective than trying to use the arms. So sink those hips and don't strangle the boom with your grip!

How low can you go?

A good way to tell that you are outboard and committed is to make sure that you can see your feet out in front rather than directly underneath.

Destroying the 7

Hunching or slouching acts like a handbrake in light winds. In strong winds it causes massive control problems.

Wrong! Putting on the handbrake by forgetting the number 7.

Launching & Landing

Launching in stronger winds and rougher waters requires a higher degree of control, timing and often quick reactions. But first you need to get your kit down to the beach safely, that alone can be tricky when it's windy, especially if it's a long distance to the water.

Safety first
- Carrying the board by holding the mast base and front foot strap uses the wind to help lighten the board.
- Carry the rig with the mast pointing into the wind and walk with the mast base facing forward.
- Never leave your rig unattached.
- Make sure your board is left on the shoreline with fin down and tail into wind.
- Make sure the rig lies downwind of the board.

Carrying board and rig together
With the wind blowing approximately side on to the board, stand in the gap between the board and the rig. Lift by gripping the footstrap (forearm against the deck) and boom (just near harness line) while pulling the board and rig close into the body.

Board above the head

In more marginal wind or to get out through the initial shore break, it is possible to carry a board and rig 'above your head'. First position the board side-on to the wind.

Place the front hand just below the boom on the mast or right up by the mast at the front of the boom – whatever you feel most comfortable with. Bend your knees and allow the rig to drop back onto your head, until it is almost horizontal.

With the rig raked back resting on your head, the nose of the board should start to lift. At this point grip the front strap and tuck the elbow in close to your body.

As you stand up, you must keep the rig raked back and as horizontal as possible. This often requires a little shuffle with your head to find a 'comfortable' balance point for the rig.

Top Tip
For control, keep the whole set-up side on to the wind, which is fine when walking forwards or backwards. To move left or right, adopt a 'crab like walking action' shuffling sideways with your feet to keep the rig roughly side on to the wind.

Learning to launch in a shore break

Ideally find a gently shelving beach, with a side shore wind and avoid high tide. In onshore conditions, watch others first to work out which is the favourable tack to leave the shore on. Keep the board and rig clear of the water until you're about knee depth. Once in the water you can hold the mast and tail of the board to position the board. When you've let go of the board, hold the rig well clear of the water. Stand slightly to windward of the tail. As soon as possible, get both hands on the boom.

Beachstart in a shore break

When you see a gap in the waves, make your move. The temptation is to step up straight onto the board, but this is exactly where it goes wrong. You need good forward motion! So don't be afraid to walk, step and actually push the board forward as you move onto it. Approaching from the back towards the front (roughly in line with the leeward front footstrap), rather than stepping on sideways onto the board like a bench creates far more speed.

5 key points

VISION – First look for the smoothest water, then get that head rolling in towards the mast base.
TRIM – Make sure the back foot lands on the board between the front and back straps, with heel on the windward side of the board (and toes pointing slightly forward).
BALANCE – Force the rig well forward and sink the body low and forward momentum reduces the risk of being pulled over the front.
POWER – To create 'lift' from the rig the front arm should be forced up and forwards as the backhand sheets the boom in above your head. Pull down hard on the boom only when you're up and moving forward.
STANCE – 'Nose over toes'. As you come up onto the board, really flex that back leg rolling your head inboard below the boom and towards the mast base. The front foot is last to come up and should be placed right up by the mast base.

Bend your leg!
If you try to stand straight up on the board by pulling down on the rig, the board will stall and not drive ahead. To avoid this problem, keep your back leg well bent with your foot on the board and push through your well extended front leg.

Top Tips
When the board is hit by an oncoming wave or large piece of chop, flex both legs to absorb the impact, keeping low to prevent the rig pulling you over the front.

- If you drop the rig in the water, elevate it by sliding the mast to windward and upwards. If you just try to lift the mast, the clew often gets caught in the water and turns the rig over.
- Never stand with the board or rig directly between you and breaking waves.
- As a wave approaches, always keep the nose pointing directly into the wave by pushing forward through the boom and down onto the mast base.
- If you lose control of the board and rig in bigger breaking waves, or if you're suddenly out of your depth, go to the mast tip, hold it tight, and swim into the oncoming waves to prevent the board being swept away from you.

Coach's Corner

What's going wrong?

Why do I get pulled over the front of the board?

The board is pointing too far downwind or is too 'sideways on' to the waves.

Why do I spin into wind?

This could be a combination of too much weight on the tail, positioning the rig too far back, or trying to get away when you're too side-on to the board. Make sure you push through the front foot to drive the nose of the board away.

Coming back to the shore

Head upwind to reduce speed, pull down on the boom and step off to windward with the front foot first. Hold the mast with your front hand and grab the back strap with the back hand. This helps keep the rig flying and the fin clear of the water as you walk back to the beach. Never stand with the board between yourself and an oncoming wave.

Uphauling

The better you get, the more you'll need to uphaul. Strange, but true. Firstly, if there's suddenly insufficient wind to waterstart and you're out on a small board you will have to uphaul. This becomes very common once you venture into higher wind environments. Secondly, even in planing conditions, if the rig is lying downwind, it's often far quicker and much less effort to uphaul rather than go through a time consuming waterstart.

Uphauling side-on to the wind (beam reach) with your feet across the board in a 'secure position' might work in zephyr winds on flat water. Yet when you encounter waves or high winds it causes great instability, because the board rocks from side to side.

Point board towards wind and pull rig forward.

Tilt the board to windward for greater stability.

Keep weight forward as you grasp the rig with one hand.

Pull to windward and sheet in.

Uphaul into the wind

Try turning the board slightly upwind of a beam reach, so the board points more into the wind and the chop. This increases overall stability and encourages the rider to pull the rig from the back of the board, and then forward, which makes it much easier to sheet in without falling off.

Placing your front foot on the windward edge and tilting the board as you uphaul adds extra leverage and takes so much of the strain out of initially raising the rig. Should the board ever sink, work on keeping the board flat. Even if you're up to your knees in water it's possible to remain stable.

Top Tip

- On narrower Freeride, or on Freestyle and Wave boards where the footstraps are more central and forward, slip the back foot (the wrong way) into the leeward front strap. This creates far greater leverage, control and more stability, especially if the board is small enough to submerge.

Sailing Upwind off the Plane

Whenever you leave the beach, or before you want to get planing, always head upwind first. This helps to sheet the rig in, so you can spot lulls and gusts, with your feet forward to promote early planing.

VISION – Head up, shoulders back and look forward.

TRIM – The front foot goes in line with the mast base, but right on the windward side and on this occasion you need to dig the rail into the water. The rear foot goes to windward of the centre line, just in front or behind the front strap.

BALANCE – Initially the rig is raked back to turn the board into wind, then it is brought to just forward of upright to power the board. The front arm must extend and push the mast downwind as the body counter-balances gently to windward.

POWER – Have your boom high enough to sheet in and back and pull down on the boom.

STANCE – The front leg and arm extends to form a Straight 7 stance with the hands just either side of the harness lines to keep the rig away from the body.

Top Tip

Be quite gentle on the rig and don't put excessive weight on the back foot, otherwise the board just goes sideways.

Coach's Corner

Dig the rail in and grip the water

If the board is not planing, you will have to creep slowly upwind. Digging that rail gives extra lateral resistance.

Mastering Harness & Footstraps

Compared to your initial experiences of getting into the harness and footstraps on higher volume boards in marginal winds, getting into the harness and footstraps on smaller boards is all about exaggerating the elements of the Formula.

Gear Check

As wind speed increases and board volumes reduce, the need for your gear to be set up correctly and work with rather than against you is essential.

Harness fit
Make sure the harness hook is very tight, with hardly any up, down or sideways movement of the bar.

Harness line positioning
It is impossible to state exactly where the harness lines should go before getting on the water. The bottom line is that you should always be prepared to fine tune harness line width (between your hands) and length (from boom to hook) while out on the water. The objective is to create a good distance between the boom and the upper body to improve your balance and stance. Always start with the fixing points at just a maximum hand's width apart, but you can go even narrower for wave and freestyle sailing.

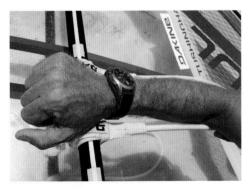

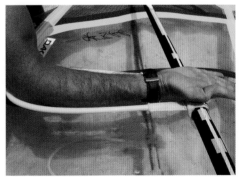

Elbow to watchstrap
A range of elbow to watchstrap usually favours seat harness users.

Elbow to palm
Elbow to "chicken leg" part of palm usually favours waist harness users.

Remember – waist harnesses need longer lines

If the lines are too short, it means that the upper body is pulled too close to the boom, causing bent arms and a poor stance.

Rule of hands

This is a very rough guide for sails between 5-7m in light-marginal powered conditions. Match the number of clenched hands to the sail size and count them down the front of the boom (by the boom clamp). For instance count five hands down the boom for a 5m rig or six hands down the boom for a 6m rig. This provides a starting point to progress from as hand sizes vary. You may find the position is too far forward.

Rule of thirds

Run a tape measure from the clew of the sail to the middle of the mast. The rear harness line fixing goes one third of the way down the boom. This favours a fully powered rig.

Rig lift

This is an amazingly simple way to set up a good pre-sail position, which is quite close to the one-third rule. Find a sheltered area, out of the wind and lift the rig with one or two fingers. If the clew drops, move the lifting point back towards the clew. If the mast drops, move the lifting point forward towards the mast. If the boom remains level when you lift it, position the harness lines just either side of this point. On the water you rarely have to adjust the lines more than a few centimetres from this point.

Fine Tuning Harness Lines on the Water

Perfect set-up

Sail along fully sheeted with the clew just over the leeward side of the tail. Then, momentarily, put both hands over your harness lines. The rig should remain stable with equal pressure on each arm.

Harness lines too far forward

If the back arm feels more pressure or the apex of the line is angled towards the tail, this indicates that the lines need to move further back along the boom.

Harness lines too far back

If the front arm feels more pressure, the front leg constantly bends or the apex of the harness line is angled towards the nose, move the lines forward along the boom.

Formula Skills for Harness & Footstraps

VISION
Look forward, not at the harness line or footstraps. Sail across the wind in marginal winds and head upwind in challenging conditions.

TRIM
Make sure both feet are on the windward side of the centre line. Adopt a narrow foot spread in lighter winds and a wide spread in stronger winds. Make sure each foot is right next to the respective foot strap before trying to put your foot in it.

BALANCE
Front Strap: Remember the basics – rig forward and body back to un-weight the front foot.
Back Strap: Head upwind, rake the rig back and lean the body forward to un-weight the back foot.

POWER
Sink down hard in the harness to keep that rig sheeted in.

STANCE
In virtually all situations, being strong and extending through the front arm and leg, creates greater stability, enhances trim and makes it easier to sheet the rig in and maintain speed and control.

- In marginal winds adopt a Straight 7 lift and lock stance before getting into the harness and straps.
- In stronger winds adopt a Super 7 drop and dig stance to emphasis power, trim and control acceleration.

Strong Wind Harness Techniques

Look forward and sail upwind before hooking in. This encourages the rig to sheet in and reduces the chances of being pulled over the front of the board.

With the front arm extended, drop down into a Super 7 stance and pull in, back and down on the boom, while bringing the harness lines to windward. In stronger winds really accentuate this action!

Once hooked in, relax the arms, hold the rig still and sit down in the harness to keep pressure down through the line.

Top Tips
- Move the hands up and down the boom to get more comfortable and avoid a strangulation grip!
- In medium to strong winds adopt a shoulder width grip.
- In marginal winds, adopt a narrow grip.

Using the Footstraps

Getting into the straps in stronger winds requires determination, the right sailing line and a workable strategy, much of which evolves around counter-balance and a good stance.

Front strap technique: rig forward, body back

Once in the front strap, correct your stance, settle and maintain speed to prepare for the back strap.

VISION: Sail across the wind, or slightly upwind if well powered up.

TRIM: Place the front foot just forward of the front strap. The back foot goes just behind the front strap in lighter winds or towards the back strap in stronger winds.

BALANCE: To move the front foot, sit back and down over a bent back leg. Oppose this movement by forcing the rig forward by extending the front arm.

Back strap technique: rig back, body forward

Slide the back foot from the windward rail and into the strap, with rig raked back and body leaning forwards.

VISION: Look forward and head upwind 5-15 degrees above a beam reach.

TRIM: Place the back foot next to the back strap, with the heel on the windward rail.

BALANCE: Rake the rig back towards the tail and lean forwards to un-weight and slip the back foot in the strap.

Once in the back strap, establish a strong stance and bear away if you've lost speed by forcing the rig forward.

POWER & **STANCE** for front and back straps.
- Keep the weight in the harness and don't pull the boom too close to the body.
- In marginal winds, adopt a Straight 7 stance.
- In stronger winds drop and dig towards a Super 7 stance.

Top Tips
- Avoid looking at the harness line, rig or straps.
- Make sure the strap is open enough to get all the toes right through.
- Most importantly, try to adopt a good stance and keep the rig sheeted in before, during and after going for the harness and straps.

Early Planing & Pumping

VISION: Head up, shoulders back and look forward. Sail 5-15 degrees off a beam reach.

TRIM: Front foot just to windward of the mast base pointing forward. Rear foot goes next to, or even in front of the front straps in very light winds, with heel to windward of the centreline.

BALANCE: The front arm fully extends to push the mast forward, which increases the power of the rig, assists trim and allows your body to angle back.

POWER: Position your boom high enough to sheet the boom in, back and down.

STANCE: Initially adopt a Super 7 drop and push stance to lean back and drive the board forward. Once the board starts planing adopt a Straight 7 prior to and after hooking in.

Early planing means more quality sailing and reduces the reliance on larger sails. Getting your board going before everyone else is always down to good technique. People assume you just sail off downwind to get planing, but often end up standing too far back on the board with the sail sheeted out. So always head upwind first, looking forward and upwind for gusts. This sheets the rig in and enables you to bring both feet forward to trim the board flat prior to bearing away. Remember that you need more wind to get going in the harness than out of the harness, so hooking-in too soon will reduce the chances of accelerating away.

Pumping onto the plane

In marginal conditions sail no more than 5-15 degrees downwind of a beam reach to promote planing. The instant you feel a decent gust, adopt a Super 7 drop and push stance, rig and feet forward, to encourage the shoulders back and to windward.

To pump, keep the lower body **still** whilst sheeting the rig in hard with the back hand and then scooping the mast forward at the end of each the pump. Think *'Clew in, mast forward.... clew in, mast forward..... clew in, mast forward'*. Try to keep the hips and legs locked to drive the board **flat** and forward. As the board planes, hook in and quickly establish a Straight 7 stance by 'lifting and locking' the hips and tightening the torso.

Once in the front strap change the counter balance by raking the rig back and leaning the body forward. This enables you to stay sheeted in, maintain trim and makes it easier to slip into the back strap.

Rolling onto the leading ledge of your front foot enables you to lean forward without having to flex the front leg too much.

Coach's Corner

Don't hunch up

Hunching and pulling on your arms too much, destroys early planing. Grip the boom lightly. Try using three fingers, rather than a death grip. Think harness not hands. The rig will act like a brake and stall the board if you hunch up, pull too hard on the boom, put too much weight on the back foot or sheet out too far. The rig acts like a brake and stalls the board.

Top Tips

- If the water ahead has dark patches indicating wind, bear away to accelerate.
- If the water ahead looks windless head upwind to pick the next gust.

Blasting Control & Steering

Rougher water, higher speeds and more sensitive boards often compound control problems. The good news is that they are all solvable and stronger winds can be a real joy. First off, it is vital to ensure your gear is set up correctly. Lack of control is not helped by over or undersized boards, fins, or poorly tuned sails.

Your objective is to keep the board flat (TRIM) and the rig sheeted in (POWER). Commitment and exaggerating the Super 7 drop and dig stance play a huge role in your success.

VISION: Look forward to spot chop and rough water.
TRIM: Pull up on the toes and dig those heels down, especially with your front foot. Heavily flexing the back leg reduces nose lift at speed.
BALANCE: Directly oppose the rig, massively weighting the harness. Also, keep your distance from the mast with a strong extended front arm.
POWER: Accentuate pulling in, back and down on the boom to help trim.
STANCE: All of the above assist a Super 7 drop and dig stance, where the front leg remains extended and the rear leg flexes.

How should I control excessive speed?
Accentuate the Super 7 drop and dig stance, by sinking your hips down, back and to windward in the harness. This emphasizes POWER and enables you to drive through both legs, digging your heels down onto the windward rail to improve TRIM. Sometimes this requires the upper body to hunch slightly.

Changing course at speed
When you're blasting flat out, it is beneficial to be able to steer, avoid others and take the board where you want it to go. It only takes the slightest pressure to alter course. The more outboard you are, the easier it is to oppose the movement of the rig and push and pull through the legs to change the direction of the board.

Upwind Steering – Super 7 drop and dig (picture 1)

Just looking over the front shoulder at speed is often enough to turn the board upwind. If you also pull up on the toes and dig the heels, especially the front foot, you'll weight the windward rail and head upwind. If this is insufficient, apply additional weight to the back leg/foot and momentarily rake the rig towards the tail.

Downwind Steering – Super 7 drop and push (picture 4)

Turning downwind onto a broad reach is worth practising for planing entries into gybes. Push through the toes of an extending front leg and flex the back leg. If this is insufficient to make the board bear away, force the rig forward a little. Make sure you are pulling down on the boom and your body is low and back, with the rear leg flexed.

Coach's Corner

What happens when things go wrong?

How do I cope with chop and stop the board leaping out of the water?

The moment you sense or feel the nose lift over chop, accentuate your Super 7 stance and flex that back leg heavily. This absorbs the punch from the chop and brings the nose back down should you unintentionally get air!

How do I get over small waves?

Head upwind on the approach. The moment you feel the whole board lift up the wave, accentuate your Super 7 stance while flexing both legs heavily to absorb the impact of the wave. Should you get airborne, keep low, tuck the back leg in towards your body and extend the front leg forward as your hips sink back towards the tail.

Why can't I hook in?

This is often due to sailing too far downwind or sheeting out too far. Head upwind and sheet in prior to hooking in.

Why do I keep heading up into wind?

This is usually due to too much weight on the back foot, sheeting out, leaning the rig too far back, standing up or bending both arms too much.

Why do I get pulled over or catapulted by the rig?

You're sailing too far downwind, your feet are too far forward or inboard, or perhaps there's not enough weight pulling down in the harness.

Why do I end up missing the foot strap?

Place your foot right next to the strap and slide toes across the deck. Don't stab at it.

Why do I spin out?

At high speeds over choppy water or if you get 'air' the fin can lose grip and 'spin out' with the board sliding sideways. This is due to either a sudden change of direction, the windward rail lifting excessively or over-weighting on the back leg. To recover from spinning out, stand up slightly to un-weight the tail, sheet the sail out slightly and then pull or 'snap' the tail in under your body to re-engage the fin.

Why do I catapult?

Avoid sailing side-on to waves, blasting too far downwind in an upright position or over straightening your back leg. Most importantly commit to that harness and keep the boom sheeted, in, back and down!

Why do I constantly head upwind?

This can be caused by too much body weight or rig movement towards the tail, maybe suddenly sheeting out, or pulling the rig too close to the body.

Get back in control

- If you feel the board is going too fast or you're losing control – be it blasting, setting up for a gybe, a jump or just wanting to regain control – *head upwind!*

Fast Tacking

Most people can tack a larger board in lighter winds, yet when it comes to tacking a lower volume board in stronger winds, the board starts to wobble and they lose all hope mid-tack! The key to tacking shorter boards is breaking the move down into key components, plus understanding that it's a misconception that you whizz from side to side around the mast. Tacking relies on vision, counter-balance and a very specific footwork, which we call Shifting and Switching.

We are not re-learning any new skills, just building from what we have already learnt during our intermediate course.

Vision to tack
Look and sail upwind before tacking.

As the nose of the board passes through the eye of the wind, move your head to look out of the turn.

Staring at your feet, hands or a moving rig causes instant imbalance. Keep your head up and look where you want the tack to finish.

Counter-balance
Most people comprehend the importance of raking the rig back going into the tack, and then throwing it forward at the end of the move. However, the movements in the middle tend to cause all the problems on shorter boards. You have to grasp the concept that the mast needs to be pushed across the board to leeward as your body shifts across to windward mid-tack. The mistake is to try and step round an upright fixed mast, which usually ends up with the mast being pulled forwards. This will destroy any counter-balance, sinking the nose and leaving little room for you to stand on the new side of the board.

Footwork: 'Shifting & Switching'

To create quick feet, you need a simple system. Practise this 3-step Shifting and Switching action on the land before going out on to the water. By spreading the feet on exit you have far more leverage to help turn the board downwind. By stepping towards the back of the board at the end of the tack, you reduce nose sink and can throw the rig forward, sheeting in with less chance of going over the front.

Entry: The front foot steps forward and wraps tightly around the mast, while the hips and rear foot shift forwards. This helps move the rig back and body forward.

Mid: As the board heads into wind, bring the hips forward **and turn them to face down the board**. Make your move by switching the back foot behind the front foot. Rig moves to leeward and body to windward.

Exit: As soon as the board comes out of the tack, the old front foot steps as far down the board as possible. Rig forward and body back.

Coach's Corner

Don't dismount when you tack
Dismounts are created by pulling the rig too close to your body; moving in the same direction as the rig, not moving your feet or staring at your wonderful board.

Why do I fall into windward with the sail before I get round the mast?
Because your hips and back foot are not far enough inboard and towards the mast base.

Why does the nose sink and I fall off the front?
Check your feet are not too far forward. You may also be pulling the rig forward mid-tack.

Why do I get to the other side and fall in with the sail on top of me?
The board has not turned far enough through the wind or you have not pushed the mast sufficiently downwind mid-tack.

ENTRY

Vision: Look and sail upwind, unhook and come out of the straps. As you rake the rig back, place your front hand on the mast, or on the boom right up by the mast.

Shifting & Switching: The front foot must step forward and wrap around the mast base before the board is head to wind.

Counter-balance: As the board sails upwind, move your body and rear foot forward and inboard. It's important to keep the rig raking movement going, so that the clew crosses over the tail of the board. This indicates that you're passing through the eye of the wind. At this point, set up the move by edging your hips inboard so they face towards the *back* of the board, *before* making your move to switch the feet.

MID TACK: These next points happen virtually simultaneously.

Vision: Once the board passes right through the eye of the wind, look out of the turn and grab the boom on the new side.

Shifting & Switching: The old back foot switches behind the front foot.

Counter Balance: It is essential to *push the mast to leeward as you switch the feet and move the body to a windward position!*

Balance: The old mast hand is released once the new front is placed well down the boom. Now quickly step as far back on the board as possible and force the rig forward to counter-balance.

EXIT

Vision: Look out of that turn!

Super 7: Adopt a wide foot spread and pull the clew hand (back hand) in hard to push and turn the board downwind! Drop and Push to make the board bear away.

Top Tip
- Never try and tack unless the clew has passed over the tail of the board to leeward, or there will be no room for you on the new windward side!

Cracking Waterstarts

The gateway to sailing smaller boards and enjoying stronger winds, waterstarting is a key stage in becoming a more accomplished windsurfer. It's a mechanical action that is often taught to fast progressing beginners before they master harnessing and straps. So don't put it off, because waterstarting has very little to do with your blasting ability. With the right guidance, it doesn't take long to master flying the rig, after which the process of rising up onto the board involves exaggerating the key skills from a beach start.

Waiting for lift-off...

Board & rig positioning

You need to align the mast across the wind before trying to elevate the rig out of the water, which can be done in two ways.

With the board side-on to the wind, it's possible to slide the mast across and over the tail and then up to windward.

Alternatively, point the nose of the board into wind with the mast at right angles to the board before trying to elevate the rig.

Rig elevation

Get yourself a good distance upwind from the mast by extending your arms. Give the mast/luff a good shake to release some of the surface tension. Initially keep the mast horizontal, but start to swim your body and rig to windward by kicking with your feet under the water. As the rig starts to move, make a really strong positive *sliding* action with your front arm to pull the mast from a downwind position. You should pull the mast towards, over and well past your head in a windward direction.

Keep the rig as horizontal as possible, only lifting the mast up when it has passed right over your head and the clew is clear of the water. Once the rig and clew are free, grab the boom well past the rear harness line with the back hand and quickly transfer the front hand onto the boom.

Top Tip

- Don't try to lift or push the mast straight up too soon. This will push you down or make the clew of the sail drop and catch in the water.

Clew catching

If the clew catches in the water, immediately pull down on the mast and draw it to windward to get the rig horizontal and clear the clew. This is very counter-intuitive. You naturally want to lift the mast, but that makes the clew drag even more.

Top Tips

- When manoeuvring the rig, adopt a wide arm spread to push and pull on the mast.

- Initially keep the body well upwind of the mast and always try to pull the whole rig towards you.

- Avoid reaching under the sail and trying to grab the boom before the clew is fully clear of the water, or the clew will sink and you will be dragged downwind.

Board positioning

In strong winds aim to start your waterstarts 5-10 degrees upwind of a beam reach.

In lighter winds aim to start your waterstarts across the wind on a beam reach, or at most 5-10 degrees downwind of a beam reach.

Taking a breather

If you want to save energy or rest, position the board at 90 degrees to the wind in a neutral position by holding the mast (or boom right up by the mast) with the front hand and the rear strap with your backhand.

Steering with the rig

You want to come up onto the board in a forwards motion, roughly in line with the leeward front footstrap. Don't try to come up side-on to the board, because this will spin you into wind or you'll just drift sideways. Steer the board with the rig to make sure you are in the right place at the right time.

Here's how to steer prior to coming up onto the board.

Steering downwind

To turn downwind and increase power, force the mast tip to windward and forward by pushing forward on the front hand and pulling in and up on the back hand.

Steering upwind

To turn upwind and reduce power, force the mast tip to leeward and back towards the tail by pulling in on the front hand and pushing out on the back hand.

Fanning the rig for precision steering

Keep your feet directly beneath your body and 'fan' the clew in and out with the back hand. This makes steering much easier and reduces the chances of you being pulled about by the rig.

Angle to the wind

Position the board across the wind, or slightly upwind in stronger winds, with your body just upwind of the tail.

Rig twisting

When you're ready to generate extra 'lift', extend your front arm up and forward, simultaneously pulling the back hand in towards and then above your head. This feels like turning a set of giant handle-bars *above your head*. It creates a 'twisting action' that generates lift and needs to be accentuated in marginal winds. Raise the rig as high as you can *before* bringing the back foot (facing slightly forward) up on the board between the straps, with the heel just to windward of the centreline.

Once you've made contact, really flex the back leg to pull the tail in towards your body as you continue to extend and twist the rig as high as possible. As you do so, roll your head inboard below the boom and towards the mast base. Leave bringing the front foot up as late as possible.

Once you're up on the board, adopt a really low Super 7 position, pushing through the forward placed front foot to stop the board luffing.

Rig recovery

Invariably the board and rig end up facing the wrong way, so it's vital to learn these three tricks to get out of any situation.

Rig downwind

Rather than lifting the clew and sinking the mast to turn a rig over, just stand on the end of the boom and pull on the uphaul. This takes far less effort and drains the luff.

Coach's Corner

Waterstart Problems

Why do I get pulled over the front?

The board is pointing too far downwind or your body has swung 'outboard' and forward, which is often due to an over-extended back leg.

Why do I fall back into the water?

Be careful not to pull or bend your arms too much or stand up too soon. Also avoid lifting the hips up excessively or bringing the front foot up onto the board too soon.

Why do I keep heading up into wind and/or falling off the back?

More aggression is needed to keep the mast forward. Make sure your back leg is not too straight or over-weighted. Do not try to waterstart with the board too far into wind.

Fly the rig: One of the most valuable tricks is to fly the rig and then turn the board and gybe the sail. The secret is to keep the boom level and make sure the mast is angled more towards the tail before releasing and rotating the rig.

Top Tip
- If the rig is either directly to windward, you're in waves or struggling to elevate a large cambered sail, you can go to the very tip of the mast to fly the rig. But you still need to keep the luff into the wind as you work your way down towards the boom.

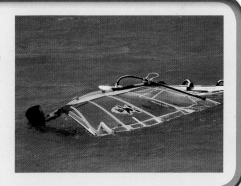

Planing Carve Gybe

A combination of continuous commitment and good timing, every successful gybe is well earned. Just like the non-planing carve gybe in RYA Intermediate Windsurfing, a planing carve gybe relies on good use of principal skills including vision, counter-balance, well timed Shifting and Switching of the feet, a controlled Rig Rotation and of course a Super 7 drop and push stance for the entry and exit of the gybe.

The major difference between non-planing and planing gybes is learning how to unhook at speed without losing control of the rig/clew and increasing the commitment to the inside rail to 'bank' the board through the turn. With everything happening quite quickly, it is very difficult to remember different points through the turn. Learning to gybe by 'giving it a go' on a windy day is why it can take some people years to learn to gybe. You need a strategy! Break the move down into distinct sections and focus on mastering them one at a time. Be prepared to use lighter winds, land routines and training exercises to simulate the actions time and time again. For best learning conditions seek flat water in nicely powered conditions.

Fundamental skills
We constantly rely on good vision and counter-balance throughout the gybe. Plus we must adopt a committed Super 7 drop and push stance for the entry and exit of the move. Three more skills are absolutely fundamental to successful carve gybes:

Unhooking – How to set up and maintain control prior to carving.

Shifting & Switching – For effective carving, a reliable foot change and counter-balance during the middle section of the gybe.

Rig Rotator – To control the forces, position and movement of the rig during the middle section of the gybe.

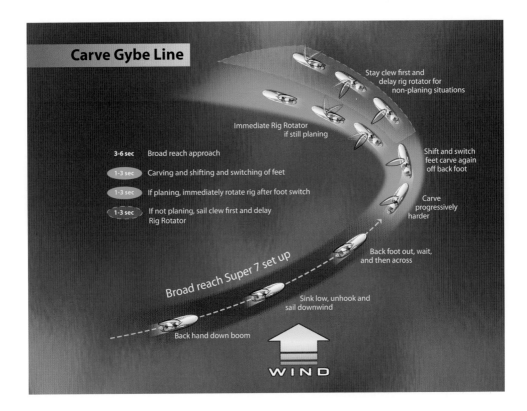

Carve Gybe Line

Stay clew first and delay rig rotator for non-planing situations

Immediate Rig Rotator if still planing

3-6 sec	Broad reach approach
1-3 sec	Carving and shifting and switching of feet
1-3 sec	If planing, immediately rotate rig after foot switch
1-3 sec	If not planing, sail clew first and delay Rig Rotator

Shift and switch feet carve again off back foot

Carve progressively harder

Broad reach Super 7 set up

Back foot out, wait, and then across

Sink low, unhook and sail downwind

Back hand down boom

WIND

The diagram shows the approximate timing and sequence of events for a planing carve gybe. You want to aim for a fast broad reach entry with a fast broad reach exit. If you have speed on the exit, you rotate the rig immediately after changing the feet. If you slow down, delay the rig rotation, sail clew first for the last part of the turn and then rotate the rig.

Whilst it's one continuous move, we've broken the gybe down into three stages to enable you to work on each key skill at a time.

How to Unhook for the Gybe

We usually unhook to slow down or stop. This engrained habit leads the gybe, causing people to stand up and sheet out when they unhook in preparation for a gybe, causing loss of speed, control and causes problems later in the turn. What's needed is a very specific and committed unhooking process, using body weight rather than strength. The objective is to sail fast, unhook and take your back foot out of the strap with the rig hardly moving from its blasting position.

- Look behind and downwind for flat, clear water.
- Sink down low into a Super 7 drop and push stance (hips just off the water).
- Extend and push through the front leg, flexing the rear leg to encourage the board to take a broad reach sailing line.

- Move the back hand well down the boom.
- Sink harder in the harness and pull in and *down* on the boom to unhook.
- Lower your Super 7 stance to stay fully sheeted in through body weight.
- Don't come up or think about carving, just accentuate POWER by hanging down off the boom.
- Take the back foot out of the strap and place it on the windward side of the board.

- Keep focused on remaining outboard, sheeted in and on a broad reach sailing line.
- From an outboard position, slide the back foot over to the leeward rail, with toes right on the rail next to the back strap.
- On very wide boards, this might require you to come up very slightly by flexing the front leg and sheeting in on the back hand.

- Start to turn downwind, *but crucially don't throw your body over into the turn too quickly*. Concentrate on sheeting in hard on the back hand and keeping the mast forward with the front arm. *Gradually* move the hips across and over the rear foot to depress the leeward rail to initiate the carve.

Top Tips

- Avoid standing up, sheeting out and rushing, coming over to carve too quickly. This kills speed in light winds and control in stronger winds.
- On very wide boards, it might require two steps to get to the leeward rail. Turning well downwind makes the turn easier.

Shifting and Switching – A key skill that is required just as the board approaches and passes the dead downwind stage of the gybe.

Shifting	**Switching**	**Switched**	**Super 7**
The carving back foot should *always* be placed with toes on the inside rail, just next to the back strap. This helps the rear hip to shift sideways across the board, over the back foot and into the turn, with your legs flexing at the knees and ankles. Try to keep the shoulders back to resist the pull of the rig.	With the hips 'shifting' into the turn, the mast is kept forwards and leant out of the turn to counter-balance. As the board just passes the dead downwind stage of the gybe, the old front foot switches across the board (heel to toe) in front of the carving back foot.	Once the new back foot has switched across to the new side, the new front foot immediately starts to move forward.	It's imperative to shuffle the new back foot back and out to the windward rail to maintain carving pressure. Adopt a Super 7 drop and push stance to maintain pressure on the windward rail to continue carving and create a dynamic stance to collect the rig and sheet in.

Coach's Corner

Make sure it's perfect every time

Practise this Shifting & Switching action on the land and during non-planing carve gybes until you can do it perfectly without looking at your feet. If the back foot doesn't switch across, you lose that carving action and seriously hinder your Rig Rotator.

Rig Rotator

- If you've come off the plane after the foot change, keep the power on by sailing 'clew first' out of the gybe on a broad reach **and then** rotate the rig.

- If you are still planing, rotate the rig immediately the new front foot hits the deck, drop low and complete your Rig Rotator.

Clew Control	**Rig Release**	**Hand Change**	

With the feet switched, look out of the turn to where you want to go. The clew arm (left in pic) pulls in and down on the boom, sheeting the clew in to split the board in half with the sail. Drop low into your Super 7 stance on a broad reach before rotating the rig.

You must slide the front hand right up towards the mast before releasing the back hand. As the boom swings over the nose, rather than trying to hold the mast bolt upright, the mast hand guides and rotates the rig in a 'scooping' action.

The old back hand passes under the old front arm and grabs the boom on the new side. The new front hand can go either under or over grip on the boom, but ideally slide it down the boom near the forward harness line fixing. The action of scooping and rotating the mast back and then forwards (not to windward) brings the boom inboard and makes it easier to sheet the sail in.

Super 7 exit
To finish, the body sinks back into a Super 7 stance to oppose the forward motion of the rig.

Top Tip
Rig across the board

- Just before and then during the foot change, sheet the rig so that it's approximately 90 degrees to the board, on a broad reach sailing line coming out of the gybe.

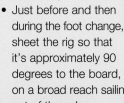

Top Tips

- Look forward, not at the rig!

- In windy conditions, rotate the rig on a broad reach to take the 'whack' and pressure out of the rig release and prevent sudden luffing.

- Standing upright and near the mast to reach for the boom, often leads to sheeting out or pulling the rig over to windward. Sinking low and back and driving off the back foot helps bring the rig to you and sheeting in.

Coach's Corner

Rig back, body forward

If the foot change and rig change are too late, the board comes too far round into wind. This is a very precarious position, which makes it much harder to sheet in and also seriously reduces your chances of planing out of a turn. To save this situation the body has to come forward to oppose the swinging towards the tail.

Rig forward, body back

To enhance planing exits, change your feet early and follow with an early Rig Rotator. Sit back to windward to keep carving the board and collect the rig. In this situation the rig is swept first towards the tail, but is then quickly whipped forward to sheet in.

Planing Carve Gybe

Component skills of a perfect gybe – vision & sailing line

Broad reach approach in controlled conditions.

Sink low and move your back hand down the boom. Unhook, keep low and just sail.

Back foot out, momentarily on the windward side, then slide it to leeward.

Stay well outboard and sheet in on the back hand hard. This helps keep the board flat as it bears away. As the board turns downwind flex the knees and ankles and keep sheeting in.

As the board approaches the dead downwind part of the turn, sheet out so that the rig is approximately 90 degrees to the board and then start Shifting and Switching the feet.

Shifting & Switching

Head near clew hand, pulling down on boom with shoulders back and carving hard off the back foot!

Keep the rig forward, sit back, flex the knees and ankles and switch the old front foot in front of the carving back foot.

Step forward, with the new front foot but keep the hips low and back.

REMEMBER: If you're at full speed, rotate the rig immediately the front foot hits the deck. If you've lost speed, sail clew first on a broad reach, then rotate the rig.

Rig Rotator

Make sure the old front hand is right up to the mast. Look out of the turn!

The rig is leant downwind, the body sinks to windward to counter-balance. Keep looking out of the turn!

Scoop and rotate the mast back and then forwards to help sheet in. Look out of the turn!

Super 7 Exit
Sink low into a Super 7 drop and push stance to collect the rig and power away.

Coach's Corner

Common gybing problems

Standing up too straight and/or sheeting out too far reduces stability and makes controlling the rig and switching the feet very difficult.

Without shifting the hips over the inside rail, the board flattens off and it's very hard to keep sheeted in. If your head is close to the front hand, you have little counter-balance, making it difficult to sheet in, switch feet and control the clew.

It is fine to lean back, but NOT if you pull the rig with you, which is a real speed and control killer.

When the feet change, keep the boom at 90 degrees to the board to give you more control prior to releasing the rig.

In stronger winds, the clew gets pulled forward, causing you to break at the waist.

Grabbing the mast with the new front hand is a speed killer. Always go boom to boom!

Slalom or Laydown Gybe

To give Step Gybes a real turbo boost, experienced gybers will exaggerate the sheeting in action after unhooking.

If you do this on a fast broad reach, you can make the sail 'go light' and 'lay' the rig lower on the water and more towards the tail. This encourages the board to turn very tightly. Note how the body leans much further forward to compensate for the rear raked rig. The hand and footwork is just like a Step Gybe but needs to be done much faster. Plus the timing and physical effort of moving the rig up, forward and then to leeward is considerable, but generates a very acute and powerful turn.

Planing exit guarantee

ENTRY: Fast, broad and sheet in! This helps lighten the rig mid turn.

MID GYBE: Change your feet early and quickly when the board is at full speed, just after the dead downwind stage of the turn. If still planing, immediately rotate the rig.

EXIT: Drop low, back and to windward. Avoid standing up to reach for the boom.

High Wind / Survival Gybe

If you're approaching a gybe and the thought of bearing away is too terrifying due to excessive wind, board speed or chop, you have another option. We call this a high wind or survival gybe. The focus is control rather than planing out. The concept is to take an upwind line rather than a downwind line when setting up the gybe. This is done to reduce board speed and help sheet the rig in. Because you're heading up into wind, it means that the board must be carved harder earlier to initiate the turn.

- In marginal or nicely powered conditions, bear away onto a broad reach during your set up. Carve later and progressively harder through the turn.

- Never just blast along and try to carve the board round from beam reach to beam reach. You will lose speed in light to nicely powered conditions and lose control in fully powered conditions. (See diagram below and sequence on page 70.)

- In over powered, choppy or challenging conditions, head upwind during your gybe set up. Be prepared to carve harder earlier in the turn. (See diagram on page 59.)

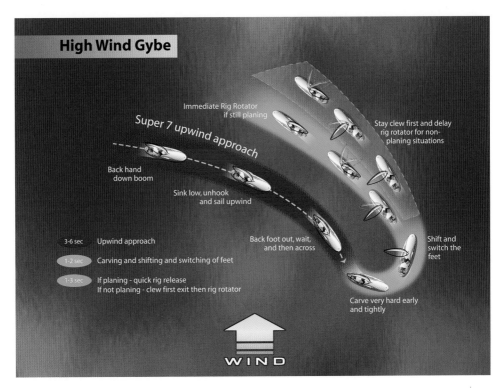

Head upwind by raking the rig back and leaning the body forward to counter-balance and trim the board flat.

The windier and choppier the water, the more you head upwind. Keep outboard and unhook as per a normal carve gybe. Lean forward more by flexing the front knee after unhooking.

Before the board comes to a stop, come inboard and sheet in and down on the boom as hard as you can on the back hand, while carving the board very tight.

Change your feet as the board just passes the dead downwind stage of the gybe.

If you have speed, release the rig after the foot change, or sail out clew first on a very broad reach to avoid being over powered.

High Wind Survival Gybe
- By heading really close to the wind, you can virtually bring the board to a stop and then 'slam gybe' the board round. You must exit on a broad reach otherwise the rig gets whipped out of your hands. Gybe from close reach to broad reach in strong winds, not beam reach to beam reach.

Strap to Strap Gybe

Also known as a 'classic' or 'wave board' gybe, the 'Strap to Strap' gybe uses a similar set up to a Step Gybe, but the rig is released and collected on the new side before the foot change. This gybe is difficult in lighter winds and on larger boards. It tends to suit very powered up wavy situations and smaller boards. A Strap to Strap gybe is worth learning, as it can save a step gybe if when the clew suddenly gets pulled out of your hands on entry.

Entry to the gybe

Set up as a normal step gybe and start to carve. As the board passes the first third of the gybe, slide the front hand up to the mast and release the back hand.

Mid gybe

Keep the mast forward and as upright as possible, angling your shoulders back and sideways into the turn.

The inside hip is driving the board through the turn and you're twisting tendons to angle the whole body round out of the turn. Carve hard!

The old back hand grabs the boom on the new side (close to the front harness line) and pulls the mast to windward and forward.

Exit from the gybe

The old front hand is released and grabs the boom to help force the rig forward. This enables the body to sit back as you release the front foot to change feet.

Top Tip
- Make sure you whip the mast forward and to windward in the middle of the turn, to avoid slowing down or dropping the rig downwind.

The Duck Gybe

If you have ever tried a carve gybe, then you have more than enough ability to try a duck gybe. It's never too early to start learning. In fact, many people can plane out of a duck gybe before they truly crack carve gybing. 50 committed attempts, under good guidance, should crack it! The secret is to master 'Ducking the sail' whilst blasting straight on a broad reach, then complete the gybe. Once you've cracked it, you can tighten up the turn.

OBJECTIVE: To make the sail go light you have to blast fast on a broad reach (20-30 degrees off a beam reach). Duck the sail and then carve the rest of the turn, leaving the foot change to the very end of the turn.

Sail fast, broad, adopt a wide grip, unhook, take the back foot out of the strap as for a gybe, but DON'T carve, just blast.

Sink solidly onto your feet, keep the shoulders back and pull the rig close to the body as you release the front hand and angle the mast forward but downwind of the board.

The released front hand grabs the boom firmly near the clew, well past the remaining back hand. Immediately release the old back hand and let the mast drop down into the turn. Crucially WAIT for a second to allow the mast to drop and swing into the turn, this helps 'present' the boom in front of your body.

Pull the rig firmly across the body and upright with the remaining back hand, as if trying to throw a ball across and then behind you.

Ideally grab the boom forward of the front harness line fixing with the front hand. But a very quick shuffle of the hands along the boom is quite common.

Coach's Corner

Duck Gybe Difficulties

Why does the rig not go light and just get ripped out of my hands?

This is either due to not pulling the rig close enough to the body before releasing the front hand or you're slowing down too much before 'going for a duck'. You need speed!

Why does the boom/mast feel too far away from me on the new side?

This is often due to leaving the duck too late and carving too far round the corner before making your move.

Skills Training

These exercises are designed to enhance your awareness, muscle memory and dramatically increase your chances of success.

Switched stance

Improves confidence moving the feet mid gybe and replicates the body position mid to end of a duck gybe. Keep the mast upright, head upwind and pull down on the boom. The back foot steps forward and then the front foot quickly steps back. Point the harness hook into wind and keep equal weight on your feet with the mast upright. Look towards the clew, sink down over the tail and sheet in with the back hand pulling towards your head. This replicates turning out of a gybe.

Nose sinks

Increases confidence and recovery options should the nose sink mid tack. Head right upwind, sheet out and slide and weight the front foot forward to sink the nose. Then sit right back by heavily flexing the back leg and sheet in to bring the nose to the surface.

Sail 360°

Simulates the hand movements for duck gybes, and means you can practise the Rig Rotator for gybe exits. Look forward, place your back hand well down the boom, keep your shoulders right back and pull the boom very close to your body before releasing the front hand, which grabs the end of the boom and allows the mast to drop downwind. Once clew first, keep the rig at 90 degrees to the board, grab and pull down on the boom on the new side. Use your Rig Rotator skills to release the boom and sail away.

Upwinders and Downwinders

Upwinders simulate beginning of tacks. Downwinders simulate ending of tacks and beginning of non-planing and tight high wind gybes. This is not 'footsteering', since it should involve full body and rig movement. Sail along and turn the board right up into using a narrower hand spread with rig back and body, feet and hands forwards. Once virtually head to wind, adopt a really wide hand and foot spread, then force the rig forward and massively move the body back with back foot near back strap. Push through the front foot and front arm and pull in hard with the back hand to sheet in, 'dragging' the rear foot under your backside to turn the board downwind.

Clew first beachstarts

Reinforces confidence and has a monumental impact on your ability to control and finish gybes.

VISION: Keep on a broad reach, making sure your back hand is well down the boom and the rig is roughly 90 degrees to the board.

TRIM: Adopt a wide foot spread on the windward side of the board. Roll your head in and below the boom as you come up onto the board. Sail away on a broad reach, pulling in and down on the boom to keep the rig roughly at 90 degrees to the board. Finish off with a nice Rig Rotator, looking forward and opposing the movement of the rig to sail away.

Non-planing carve gybe

NPCG involves key skills training exercises that also link into carve gybing.

Entry to gybe

Vision: Look into and through the turn.

Super 7 drop and push: Back hand right down the boom, then 'drop' the hips and 'push' through an extended front leg to turn the board off the wind. This is helped if the front arm extends and the back hand sheets in hard towards your head!

Mid gybe

Counter Balance: The hips are low and back, the mast is forward. As the board turns, the hips shift to the inside of the turn (over the back foot) and the mast is leant to the outside. The rear placed back hand must pull in and down on the boom, as if splitting the board in half with the rig. Don't tilt the board at low speeds. Just angle the mast, leaning it further out of the turn.

Shifting & Switching: When the board is downwind, keep pulling in and down on the boom as the foot switch takes place. Keep the clew hand near the head and look out of the turn to improve your balance.

Gybe exit

Vision: Look out of the turn as you sail clew first for a couple of seconds on a broad reach.

Rig Rotator: Slide your front hand down the boom towards the mast and then drop the hips down to counter-balance the movement of the rotating rig.

Vision: Look out of the turn, before, during and after releasing the back hand.

Super 7: 'Drop' the hips and 'push' through an extended front leg to drive the board forward.

Helicopter tacks & sail 360°

Great practice for opposing the movement of the rig, sailing clew first and completing Rig Rotators. Link into other freestyle moves such as Upwind 360's, Spocks and Flaka's.

Coach's Corner

Narrow your grip

Temporarily sail with a very narrow hand-grip using only three fingers on the boom. This helps early planing and harness line set-up. It also makes returning to a chest width arm spread feel more stable.

'Unhook and hold on'

Blast fast and practise unhooking and remaining fully sheeted in through body weight. Imperative for setting up, maintaining speed and control prior to gybes, duck gybes, jumps, loops and funky freestyle.

Flat water wave riding

Increases control for varying gybe lines and takes the mystique out of wave riding. Excellent for developing body and rig control and improving counter-balance.

Fully planing, unhooked with both feet in the straps. Blast fast and then ....

Head upwind: Rig back, body forward, narrow hand grip, weight on heels. Get ready to change the opposition and counter-balance before turning downwind.

Turning downwind: Come up over the board and whip the rig forward and windward, sliding the backhand well down the boom and sheeting in hard. Then sink the body low, back and to leeward, by heavily flexing your knees and ankles to engage and carve on the leeward rail. To head upwind again, sheet out massively with the back hand first, angling the rig back, downwind and towards the tail. Then lean the body to windward and forward, narrowing the hand-grip and sheeting out with weight on heels to turn the board upwind. Try taking the back hand off completely when you turn upwind. It puts all the emphasis on counter-balance and heel pressure!

Bump & Jump

Getting air does not require big waves or a fearless approach to your windsurfing. It's easier than learning to gybe, so if you can blast in the straps on a sub 125L board, then you should be able to pop the chop. To jump we need to momentarily reverse, much of the Formula to create the required lift! Initially you might want to drop out of the harness line for your first few attempts, but you'll soon be able to stay hooked in for small jumps as your confidence and ability grows.

Vision: Pick a small wave 5-10m ahead of you and head very slightly upwind and unhook as you approach the trough of the chosen chop/wave.
Trim: The body moves more inboard, leans back and bends the front leg to allow the nose to lift.

Trim: Move further inboard, lean right back, excessively weight and push down on the back foot as the tail reaches the trough. The front leg simultaneously bends to get wind under the nose and create more lift.
Balance & power: The front arm bends and the back arm sheets out to reduce power and take pressure off the mast base.
Stance: The body is quite upright, which should be totally opposite to your normal sailing stance.

Provided you pushed down on the trough, the board will start to release, lift and get air. There's little time to enjoy the short haul flight, so you need to prepare for the landing immediately by re-establishing the Formula.

Vision: Look forward to spot a landing.
Trim: Extend the front leg and pull the tail up tightly underneath your backside by heavily flexing the back leg.
Balance: Be very firm with the front arm to keep the mast forward.
Power: Start to sheet in to re-establish your sailing position.
Stance: Your stance should feel like a very tucked and coiled Super 7 position, pushing the board forward through the front leg to prepare beautifully for the landing. To regain speed, uncoil the Super 7 drop and push stance to drive the board flat and forwards.

Coach's Corner

Things that go wrong...

Why won't the board take off?
This is often due to hanging too far outboard and down off the boom before take off, or it's poor timing pushing down on the trough.

Why do I go over the front on landing?
You've either taken off on a beam or broad reach, not curled your body up towards the tail or sheeted out too much before landing.

Why do I spin out on landing?
You must flex that back leg in the air to prepare for the landing.

Equipment & Rigs

Board Styles

Despite the hundreds of boards on the market and the occasional blending of styles, the core board categories and their dominant characteristics aren't too difficult to work out once you have a clear understanding of what to look for in a board.

FREERIDE – *A mix of early planing and general blasting boards.*
Volume 85L-170L
Length 250-270cm Width 65-85cm
Wind 5-30 Knots
Features Flatter rockered, harder railed, more upright fins and footstrap inserts closer to the windward rail, often with double back straps.

CROSS OVER / FREESTYLE WAVE
Manoeuvre orientated boards but maintaining high wind blasting performance.
Volume 80L-110L
Wind 12-30 Knots
Length 250-270cm Width 58-68cm
Features Compared to Freerides, Cross Over/Freestyle Wave boards have a more forgiving curved rocker line, higher nose lift, softer rails and more raked back fins. These boards can be used with either inboard and single or outboard and double back straps.

FREESTYLE – *Trick orientated*
Volume 90L-115L
Wind 11-25 Knots
Length 235-250cm Width 56-68cm
Features Flat rocker lines, softer rails, usually very wide compared to boards of similar length. Flat decks, kick tails and footstraps set very inboard, forward and only ever have a single back strap option. Lilliputian sized fin. Due to very early planing and excellent gybing characteristics, they make great all round boards for flat water locations, if top blasting speed isn't your priority and you're keen to get onto smaller sails as soon as possible.

WAVE BOARDS

For high winds and a moving pitch!

Volume 70L-95L

Length 235-250cm Width 52-57cm

Wind 15-40 Knots

Features Increased rocker in both tail and nose areas, much softer rails, especially around the tail. Inboard single back strap options, smaller swept back fin and narrower tails compared to other boards.

Design Characteristics

Rocker lines

Lay a straight edge lengthways down the underside of your board and you'll find a 'flat section' under the area between the front and back straps. Tail rocker refers to how much lift or kick there is in the tail behind the flat section. Nose rocker is the amount the board lifts up in front of the flat section. Boards with less tail rocker plane earlier and go faster. Higher rockered boards are slower, but more controllable. Boards with more nose rocker ride over chop and waves better.

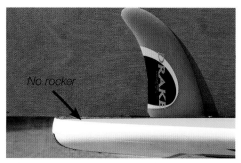

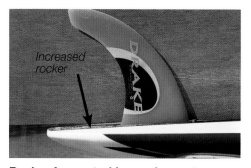

No rocker for speed and flatter water

If there is little or no tail rocker, the chances are your board will plane early compared to boards of similar size and volume with more tail rocker.

Rocker for control in rougher water

The more tail rocker your board has, the more manoeuvre orientated it will be. If you can fit your whole finger between board and straight edge, it will be slower to plane than flatter rockered boards and best suited to rougher, windier conditions.

Rail shapes

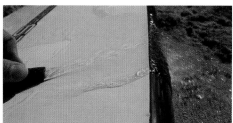

Soft rail for grip and control

Soft rails (like one side of a snooker ball) are slower but provide more grip. They feature on higher wind, good gybing and manoeuvre orientated boards. Softer rails are prominent along the rail between the straps and mast base and more towards the tail on wave boards.

Hard rail for speed and release

Sharper rails (more right angle and sharper edge) encourage the water to 'release' more easily. Early planing and fast Freeride boards have harder rails overall, particularly in the tail. Harder railed boards are usually faster and plane earlier, but are more difficult to control at speed.

Board width

Width plays a large part in how the board feels on the water. Overall width gives you stability, upwind performance and aids early planing, but generally slows top reaching speed and increases control difficulties in choppy conditions.

- Wider boards are more stable, plane earlier, plus they can carry larger fins and sails, all of which promote early planing and upwind performance.
- Wider boards tend to be bouncier in chop and harder to control when over-powered.
- Wider boards with narrow tails pivot or turn more easily.
- Narrower boards are slower to plane, plus they prefer smaller fins and sails.
- Narrower boards are far more directional and controllable in stronger winds or chop.
- Generally, heavier sailors or those looking for early planing should consider wider boards than lighter sailors or those seeking control.

Effects of volume, width, rocker & rails

If your board is either too high in volume, too wide, too flat or has excessively hard rails, you may experience some of these problems.

- The board 'flips over' when beach or waterstarting in very strong winds.
- The board's nose leaps about in the water and is impossible to keep flat over chop.
- The board takes you where 'it' wants to go.
- The windward rail lifts and your ankles are straining when blasting.
- You constantly sail upwind, even with a relatively small fin.
- The board bounces out when engaging the rail during gybes.
- Sailors of similar weight, level and sail size are in greater control especially in high winds.

Answer: Drop a few litres, narrow the board's waistline and go for more forgiving softer rails and more rocker.

If your board is too low in volume, too narrow, too rockered or has excessively soft rails, you may experience some of these problems.

- You have difficulty staying upwind, despite being powered up with a sensible sized fin.
- The board feels very sluggish to plane and slows down very quickly.
- Sailors of similar weight, sail size and ability are regularly planing more quickly or have higher top speeds.

Answer: Pile on a few litres, spread the board's waistline and go for a flatter rocker and sharper rails.

Board weight
A lighter board will plane earlier than an identical heavier board, plus it will have a more 'lively' feel on the water. However, a lighter board may not be relevant to your kind of sailing. For instance, a lighter board with lots of rocker may not get planing faster than a heavier board with very little rocker.

Go for lighter boards if you're...
- Keen on earlier planing and prepared to pump the board onto the plane.
- A good sailor and want to get on smaller boards as quickly as possible.
- Into waves, moves, feasible freestyle, flat water jumping and chucking a board about.
- A lighter weight sailor often using smaller rigs.
- Wanting one board which has to cover a wide wind or sail range.

Don't worry too much about the weight of your board if you're...
- Not prepared to pump and you prefer to hook in and rely on the wind to get you going.
- Heavy weight and only get onto your small board when it's howling.
- More concerned about control than early planing.

A true lightweight
- Always weigh the board before parting with your hard earned cash! Like humans, boards aren't always the weight they claim they are!

Board Size

Board volume guide

This is an easy guide for the majority of recreational windsurfers. You might want to fine tune to your exact needs, but it should find a board of suitable volume. If you are very new to the sport, a heavyweight or a cautious learner, go slightly bigger. If you are young, fit, pick up sports quickly or sail in very safe or shallow water, you could go slightly smaller in volume.

Take your weight in kilos (kg)	*Eg.*	*80kg*
Add rig weight when wet		*10kg*
Add board weight wet with mast base/straps/fin		*10kg*
		=100kg
Convert overall weight in kilos into litres (L).		*=100L*

Add, or subtract from this amount by including one selection from each of the following three categories.

Sailor ability

Beginner to non-planing improver ⎯⎯⎯⎯⎯⎯⎯ + 50L
Early Intermediate developing planing conditions ⎯⎯⎯ + 30L
Intermediate/Advanced (mastered waterstarts) ⎯⎯⎯ + 5L

Intended use

Wave riding ⎯⎯⎯⎯⎯⎯⎯⎯⎯⎯⎯⎯ - 10L
Bump and jump south coast style ⎯⎯⎯⎯⎯ - 5L
Freeride blasting ⎯⎯⎯⎯⎯⎯⎯⎯⎯ 0L
Feasible freestyle ⎯⎯⎯⎯⎯⎯⎯⎯⎯ + 5L
Marginal wind cruising ⎯⎯⎯⎯⎯⎯⎯ + 10L

Predominant wind conditions

Flat water/Lighter winds (9-15 Knots) ⎯⎯⎯⎯ + 20L
Medium (15-22 Knots) ⎯⎯⎯⎯⎯⎯⎯⎯ 0L
Strong (18-30 Knots) ⎯⎯⎯⎯⎯⎯⎯⎯ - 5 to15L

Sailor 80kg + board (10kg) + rig (10kg) = 100kg converted to 100L

1. Sailor Ability = Intermediate/Advanced +5L = 105L
2. Intended Use = Freeride Blasting +0L = 105L
3. Predominant Wind Conditions Medium (15-22 Knots) +0L = 105L

Total volume = 100+5+0+0 = 105L

105L is a common board size for an intermediate sailor. If you cannot waterstart, the required volume increases to approximately 130L. If you're more advanced and sailing in higher winds and waves, required volume decreases to 85-105L.

How much volume do I need to uphaul?

Take your weight in kg +10kg for the rig weight. Eg. 80kg + 10kg = 90kg
Convert that total into litres = 90L

90L is 'neutral' buoyancy for a 80kg sailor, but with practice, an advanced 80kg sailor could uphaul a 90L board.

However, if you're less experienced and want a safety margin:
Add 30-40L to be absolutely sure.
Add 10-20L if you have to uphaul in an emergency.
Add 5-15L if you might want to uphaul occasionally and you are prepared to practise it.

Do I need more volume for inland waters?
The volume variation between fresh (reservoirs/lakes) and sea water is about 2-5% depending on board size and saltiness of water. Inland sailors theoretically need 2-5L more volume than coastal sailors.

Getting Sorted

As you gain experience you're going to encounter more challenging and potentially dangerous conditions. So spend time tuning and checking your kit.

Rigging checks
- Fin bolt is fastened.
- Boom clamp, downhaul and outhaul are secure.
- Mast base, extension and uphaul are connected properly.
- Footstraps are screwed tightly and not twisting.
- Harness and lines are secure and not twisted.
- Board and rig are the right size for the conditions.

Fin Size Formula
The fin needs to be big enough to keep you upwind and planing. but not too large to cause control difficulties.

1. Recreational 'Freeride' boards 115-200L
Sail size x 5 + 4 = approximate fin size.
(E.g. 7m x 5 + 4 = 39cm fin)

2. Recreational 'Freeride' boards below 110L
Sail size x 5 + 2 = approximate fin size.
(E.g. 5m x 5 + 2 = 27cm fin)

3. Freestyle Wave, Cross Over & Wave Boards between 85L-100L
(Including Freestyle boards being used for general sailing)
Sail size x 5 = approximate fin size.
(E.g. 5m x 5 = 25cm fin)

4. Wave Boards between 70L-85L
(Including Freestyle boards being used for real freestyle)
Sail size x 4 + 2 = approximate fin size.
(E.g. 5m x 4 + 2 = 22cm fin)

Fin size

A good fin should be the right size for your ability, the wind and sail size. Make sure it's free from dents, has plenty of flex at the tip and fits well in the fin box. Increase your fin size between 1-4cm if you are:
- Under-powered, slow to plane or have difficulty staying upwind.
- Using a Freeride board with a tail wider than 40cm (add at least 4cm)
- Spinning out a lot.
- Over 85kg or heavy on your back foot.
- For exceptionally large rigs (9m+) or on boards wider than 75cm you can increase fin size by up to 10cm.

Decrease your fin size between 1-4cm if you are:
- Very over powered.
- The windward rail/nose keeps lifting.
- Under 70kg or light on your back foot.

Fin profile

Long thin, upright fins generate more lift and are better for early planing, upwind performance and straight line speed.

"Swept back", "Raked" or "Wave or Freestyle" fins generate less lift but are more pivotal and forgiving when turning.

Many freeride boards have a 'compromise' fin to give early planing lift, but sweep the leading edge back to maintain higher speed control.

Forward or back?

If you have a classic box (screwed in from under the board), the further forward the fin position the more the board will turn. The further aft the position, the more speed and directionally orientated the board will be.

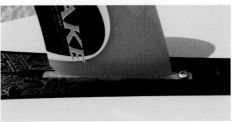

Footstrap set-up

For higher speeds, set the front strap more to the windward edge and use double back straps on wider tail boards.

Freeride

A snug fit, with the little toe just poking through. Double check the fit especially if you're wearing boots. For Wave, Freestyle Wave, Freestyle and smaller Freeride boards, set the straps more inboard with single back strap. This makes it easier to come up over the board for moves and is fine for blasting as there is less lift from a smaller fin, so no need to be so far out on the windward rail.

Wave fit

For freestyle, wave sailing and cracking moves like 360's set the straps so that the whole of the arch of your foot fits into the strap.

Mast base guide

Set the mast base to help trim the board flat! These measurements are taken from right angles of the tail to the centre of mast base and work on most modern boards.

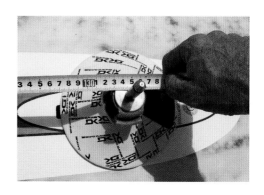

Freeride boards 115-220L
MB Range 130-145cm.
Average mast base position = 135cm from the tail.

Freeride boards 95-130L
MB Range 125-135cm.
Average mast base position = 130cm from the tail.

Freemove, Cross Over, Freestyle, Freestyle

Wave & Wave boards 75-95L
MB Range 120-135cm.
Average mast base position = 130cm from the tail.

Track tuning

- Move mast base forward (usually 1-5cm from average setting) if the tail is sinking, the board is bouncing, constantly luffing or when using max sail size.
- Move mast base back (usually 1-5cm from average setting) if the nose is ploughing through chop, or if the board feels unresponsive.

Planing boom height

Judging by the sail cutout or holding the rig up on the beach, are flawed methods. Regardless of mast base setting, you want the boom height to be set for when your feet are in the straps. The most reliable system is using the back of the board as a constant reference. An average hand's span off the back of the board just about covers the whole range of sailor heights. The taller you are within the height range the higher the boom needs to go.

- 5'0"-5'7" (1.5-1.7m) sailors would have the boom's underside within 2-8cm of the tail.
- A 5'8" (1.73m) sailor would have the boom's underside 2-6cm past the tail.
- 5'8"-6'4" (1.73-1.93m) sailors would have the boom's underside up to 6-12cm past the tail.

With wide (65cm+) Freeride boards, the boom needs to be set 3-6cm higher as you need to move further away from the centreline to get into the straps. This means it feels very high until you're blasting. To increase control for very strong winds, wave moves and freestyle you can drop the boom 1-3cm compared to your blasting / freeride setting. In non-planing situations the boom should be 'top of shoulder to chin height'.

Choosing a Sail Quiver

It's wise to plan your quiver in advance. A range of sails from the same brand should have consistent sizing and performance, possibly requiring less sails in the quiver and enabling you to get a better deal. Go for realistic differences between sail sizes. For larger rigs (over 6m) this can mean differences up to 2m's. With rigs under 6m, the size difference should be between 0.5-1.0m. Two sails with a good wind range are better than three inferior sails. Match your windsurfing to sails that have been designed for your needs.

Level/Location	Board	Stature	Number of Sails	Suggested Sizes
Intermediate/Inland	140L+	65kg	2 sail quiver	5.5m & 7.5m
Intermediate/Inland	140L+	85kg	2 sail quiver	6.0m & 8.0m
Intermediate/Inland	140L+	65kg	3 sail quiver	5.0m/6.0m/8.0m
Intermediate/Inland	140L+	85kg	3 sail quiver	5.5m/7.0m/8.5m
Int-Adv /Coastal	100-140L	65kg	3 sail quiver	4.5m/5.5m/7.0m
Int-Adv /Coastal	100-140L	85kg	3 sail quiver	5.0m/6.0m/8.5m
Int-Adv /Coastal	100-140L	65kg	4 sail quiver	4.0m/4.7m/5.3m/7.0m
Int-Adv /Coastal	100-140L	85kg	4 sail quiver	5.0m/6.0m/7.0m/8.5m
Advanced/Coastal	90-125L	65kg	3 sail quiver	4.2m/5.3m/6.5m
Advanced/Coastal	90-125L	85kg	3 sail quiver	4.7m/5.7m/7.5m
Advanced/Coastal	90-125L	65kg	4 sail quiver	4.2m/5.0m/5.8m/7.5m
Advanced/Coastal	90-125L	85kg	4 sail quiver	4.5m/5.3m/6.0m/8.0m
Wave/Freestyle	75-90L	65kg	3 sail quiver	4.2m/5.0m/6.0m
Wave/Freestyle	75-90L	85kg	3 sail quiver	4.7m/5.5m/6.5m
Wave/Freestyle	75-90L	65kg	4 sail quiver	4.0m/4.7m/5.3m/6.0m
Wave/Freestyle	75-90L	85kg	4 sail quiver	4.5m/5.0m/5.7m/6.5m

If you have one board, you can get away with a two sail quiver if you sail inland, but probably need three sails for coastal windsurfing. If you have two or more boards and sail in a wide range of conditions, then you would benefit from having three to four sails in the quiver.

Rigging and Tuning

Even the best performing sail can feel terrible if it isn't rigged well. Here's how to tune your rig.

- Slightly extend the downhaul and outhaul from the recommended mast and boom settings, usually printed on the sail.

1. Downhaul until the leech is 'loose' or 'floppy' down to the third/fourth batten. Yes, it's meant to look like this!

2. The top two battens should come straight off the centre of the mast.

3. 3rd batten down should be 35-50% rotated around the mast.

4. 4th & 5th batten should be 50-75% rotated around the mast.

Fullness & flatness
Maximum fullness is in the lower third, with the sail becoming flatter and twisting off towards the head and leech.

Outhaul
Pulling really hard on the outhaul to get the battens away from the mast usually means there is insufficient downhaul. With the correct amount of downhaul you should only need 2-5cm of outhaul.

Light/medium winds setting
Reduced downhaul and outhaul makes the sail slightly fuller, delivering more power, but reducing stability.

Insufficient downhaul
Too little downhaul is often indicated by no looseness or twist in the leech, reduces stability and control when planing.

Fully powered setting
Extra downhaul and outhaul flattens the sail, reducing power and increasing stability. It may not look that great on land, but once under tension the sail takes a great shape.

Batten tension

Tension battens to prevent creases, but not so tight that it creates S-bends.

Pulling on downhaul

Always use a spreader bar or downhaul tool and at least a 6:1 pulley to get sufficient downhaul on your rigs. If you have difficulty putting on sufficient downhaul, this action pulls the battens away from the mast and reduces friction, enabling you to apply more downhaul, but outhaul the sail first.

Rotational
4-5 battens

(no camber inducers)

Performance: Manoeuvrable, quick to waterstart and should rotate easily for tack, gybes and moves.

Suitability: Perfect all round use for virtually every board, especially for sizes 8m and below.

Wave & Freestyle Wave	Twin cam	Multi cam or Racing
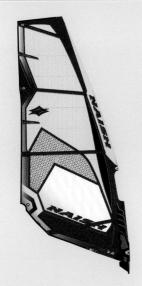		
4-5 Battens (no camber inducers)	*5-6 Battens (1-3 camber inducers)*	*6-7 Battens (3-4 camber inducers)*
Performance: Very similar to rotational sails, except they tend to have a higher aspect ratio, higher cut foot and often shorter boom for better wave clearance and moves. **Suitability**: Fine for all round use on sub 95L boards, but not quite as fast or stable for straight line blasting.	**Performance**: Tend to be more rigid, harder to rotate and very blasting orientated. **Suitability**: A consideration for rigs over 7m. Best option for sails over 8m.	**Performance**: Stiff, incredibly stable, powerful and one directional. **Suitability**: Chosen by dedicated blasters and racers only. Large luff tube is a nightmare to waterstart!

Masts and Booms

Is carbon worth the cost?

A good strong alloy boom is perfect for windsurfing. If you are using larger sails (over 7m) or want a more positive feel from your rig, carbon booms are a stronger, stiffer, but more expensive option.

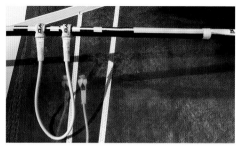

Mark the boom for clew-first moves

It's worth putting a piece of tape well down the boom to remind you to move your back hand down the boom for clew-first movements.

Skinny/RDM v conventional masts

Spotting the difference between a 75% or 100% carbon mast can be difficult. It's well worth considering Skinny or Reduced Diameter Masts on sails of 7m and below. Whilst not physically lighter, RDMs have a much lighter swing weight for tacks, gybes and waterstarts because the sail de-rotates and reduces drag. Plus, due to the extra wall thickness good Skinny masts rarely break. Virtually all modern sails work really well on a Skinny/RDM mast, so unless you're using massive rigs that are better suited to conventional diameter masts, consider switching to Skinny.

Skinny diameter masts
- Lighter to manoeuvre, de-rotate for tacks, gybes and moves.
- Easier to release for waterstarts and hold mid tack.
- Beginner–Advanced sailors all benefit. Women, lightweights and children love Skinny masts!
- Requires a skinny extension, but well worth the additional cost.

Conventional diameter masts
- Better at carrying fully powered rigs larger than 7m.
- Harder to hold, heavier to manoeuvre and more likely to break than Skinny masts.

Coach's Corner

Mast Mystique
- Due to the 'skinny effect', a 'heavier' 75% carbon Skinny mast makes the rig feel lighter than a 'lighter' 100% wide diameter mast.
- The stiffness of the mast (e.g. IMCS 25) should match the recommendations printed on your sail as closely as possible.
- Higher content carbon masts (e.g. 75-100%) are more responsive and lighter than lower content carbon masts (e.g. 30-50%).
- Once you've tried sailing with a light mast, there's no going back!

Choosing and Using a Harness

Seat harnesses enable you to sail more powered up for racing, but waist harnesses far outnumber seat harnesses in the wide windsurfing world. Overall comfort, ease of hooking in and 'freedom' of leg movement make waist harnesses an ideal choice for recreational inland windsurfers, coastal blasters, waterstarters, gybers, wave and freestyle sailors.

- Learning to use a waist harness properly forces you to adopt a decent 7 shape stance.
- With no leg straps, you must do up a waist harness tightly, with the hook just below your belly button.
- Waist harness lines need to be longer than seat harness lines to keep your upper body well away from the boom.

Elbow2Palm: Correct length lines for a waist harness, ensuring your shoulders are well away from the boom.

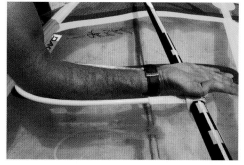

Safety & Self Rescue

As conditions become more challenging and boards get smaller, the possibilities of self-rescue become more limited. In fact many of the techniques in RYA Intermediate Windsurfing become redundant. It is vital to be aware of potential dangers and remember your seven common senses.

Seven common senses
1. Is all your equipment seaworthy and suitable? Clothing, board, rig and all essential spares.

The most common need for rescue is equipment failure!

2. Tell someone where you are going and when you will be back.

3. Obtain a weather forecast for the local sailing area.

4. Are you capable of handling the prevailing conditions?

If in doubt, don't go out

5. Windsurf with other people.

6. Avoid strong tides, offshore winds and poor visibility.

7. Consider other water-users.

When in difficulty your first action should be to attract attention and always stay with your board. If no rescue facilities are available, here are a few tips that might help you make it back to shore.

What should I do if I break a mast?
- De-rig, lie on top of your kit and paddle the board, like a surfboard.
- Ask a fellow sailor to bring out a replacement top or bottom section and re-rig your sail.
- An alternative, but very difficult solution, is to separate the broken mast and jam the mast tip into the top of the lower section so you can use enough sail to get back to the beach. This could be virtually impossible on a small board in rough conditions.

What if I break a fin?

You may be able to sail back to the beach, by tilting the board heavily to windward without sheeting right in. It's worth practising this safely in the shallows – you might need it one day!

What if I break a boom?

Reverse the boom and use the side that is still in one piece.

What if I break a UJ?

By using the 'tail' end of your downhaul or possibly even your uphaul, you may be able to tie the mast base close to the deck and then uphaul or waterstart to safety. Place a harness, wetsuit boot or deck protector under the mast base to avoid damaging the board.

What if I rip my sail?

In most cases a small rip won't prevent you getting back to shore. If the sail is unusable, you will need to de-rig and paddle.

Hitching a lift

Holding onto another sailor's board is possible for short distances, but becomes extremely hard work, especially if you're both on small boards. Try to position the boards side by side for maximum ease and efficiency.

Sailing Locations: Considerations and Advice

Wind directions

There are two main ways to describe the wind and its direction:

1. Using Points of the compass The wind direction describes where the wind is coming from. For example, a southerly wind is when the wind is blowing from the south.

2. Relative to the shoreline for example:

Off-shore
- **Wind** Blowing directly out to sea and often gusty. Feels less windy on the land than it does on the water!
- **Water** Often very flat. If there are waves, the crests 'feather' and the spray blows out to sea.
- **Launching** Launching and especially landing can be very difficult due to gusts.
- **Safety rating** Most dangerous! Easily blown out to sea!

On-shore
- **Wind** Consistent, blowing directly on to land. Often feels windier on land than on the water.
- **Water** Often 'confused' or choppy conditions.
- **Launching** Can be hard to leave shore especially with beach break at high tide.
- **Safety rating** Relatively safe, if you can get out!

Side or cross shore
- **Wind** Blows at approximately ninety degrees to the shoreline.
- **Water** Depends more on swell state.
- **Launching** Easiest conditions.
- **Safety rating** Perfect for windsurfing!

Tidal Effects and Dangers

It is easy to think that because we're skimming over the top of the water, that windsurfers are not affected by the tide. This is simply not true and there are a number of situations that directly influence our safety and enjoyment on the water. We strongly advise that you check local tides before going on the water.

Vertical movement

Vertical movement of water creates the difference between high and low tide.
Tide coming in and water is rising is called *flooding*. Tide going out and the water level is dropping is called *ebbing*.

Horizontal movement

As the tide ebbs or floods, there is also a horizontal movement of water, parallel to the coast. This can cause you to drift or be taken sideways with the tide.

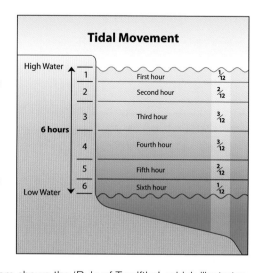

High & low

The difference between high and low water is roughly 6 hours, giving approximately 12 hours between each high tide. The tidal diagram shows the 'Rule of Twelfths', which illustrates the water flow during a given hour. The greatest movement of water is during the middle two hours and the least movement of water is either side of low and high water. Just before the tide turns, there's a short period of 'slack' water with virtually no movement. There are 24 hours and 50 minutes between daily high tides, which causes high or low water to get later each day.

Spring tides

Spring tides have the strongest gravitational pull, creating the largest tidal ranges – the lowest low tides and highest high tides, occurring every two weeks at a full and new moon.

Neap tides

Neap tides have less gravitational pull, due to occurring between a new and full moon. The tidal range of a Neap Tide is therefore much smaller.

Incoming or *flooding* tides

Going windsurfing when the tide is 'coming in' is the safest option at most coastal/harbour locations. Don't leave your gear by the water's edge for any length of time, as an incoming surge could sweep the board away. Also consider that your launching/landing area may be restricted when the tide comes in.

Outgoing or *ebbing* tides

Be very careful windsurfing anywhere in an outgoing tide, especially if the wind is in the same direction. Be aware that rocks and other obstructions may start to appear as the tide recedes. Remember that you might have a very long walk back to the car if the tide goes out a long way!

Wind and tide

Wind 'with tide', produces flatter water, but increases the chance of your board ending up downwind. The tidal flow may be fast, even though the water appears calm.
Wind 'against tide' produces rougher water, but can often act as an escalator taking you upwind.

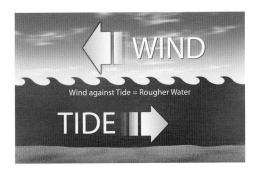

Dangerous Tidal Effects

Tidal races
There can be a considerable increase in the flow, speed and water round headlands or through narrow passages between land. When tide is against the wind, a fast moving tidal race greatly disturbs the water and can make it almost impossible to sail. It is vital to know where to avoid tidal races – check with local experts or in marine guides.

Overfall
Inconsistencies in the sea bed, reefs or even wrecks can cause the tidal flow to be uplifted, resulting in extreme disturbance on the surface.

Rip currents
Rip currents can be particularly common at wave locations, where there is a large movement of water. The geography of the shoreline can create powerful currents of water that sweep along the shore and out to sea. If a rip current is taking you out to sea, it is virtually impossible to swim back against it. You will need to swim diagonally to the direction of the current.

Where and when can I sail at high tide?
In many large harbours it is possible to windsurf a couple of hours either side of high tide. This state of tide can provide excellent flatter water blasting conditions. Windsurfing in a harbour or estuary may be an excellent choice when an onshore wind at the beach creates a difficult or dangerous shorebreak. At some locations especially on steeply shelving beaches, sailing at mid to high tide becomes increasingly harder the higher the tide gets. These conditions should be left for the very experienced/expert windsurfers actively seeking rougher conditions and breaking waves!

Where and when can I sail at low tide?
Many harbours dry out from mid to low tide, which is when a beach with an onshore wind may be most forgiving. Coastal locations tend to produce flatter shallower water areas, and even lagoons, a couple of hours either side of low tide. So if you're new to coastal sailing, then heading out at low tide is often a good option.

Shallow water moves slowly
- If you're caught in a strong tidal current, head for land and try to sail over the shallowest where tidal flow will be slowest.

Wave Sailing

For more advanced sailors, coastal locations offer the opportunity to venture into bump, jump and wavy conditions, where 'safe sailing' becomes extremely important.

Windswell

- In most locations the wave formation and height are directly related to the direction and strength of wind. Light offshore winds make the water glassy and flat; stronger on-shore and side-shore winds push up waves.
- Larger waves form, peak and start to break, in Force 4. Force 5-6 on the sea will create sizable waves with a power behind them, but when the wind drops the waves soon disappear.

Groundswell travels for hundreds of miles and produces the finest waves.

Groundswell

Tropical storms and large low pressure systems create much larger swells that can travel (propagate) huge distances. Wave size is proportional to the duration, fetch and wind strength from the source that generated the swell, with distance between crests known as 'wave length.'

Breaking waves

When windswell or groundswell reach shallow water, the bottom of the wave will start to slow due to the increased friction from hitting a reef, sand bar or shelving beach. The energy of the swell will continue forward and the wave will start to 'jack up', curl, peak and then break. Rolling energy contained in a wave extends to at least twice its face height below the surface. Therefore a wave will begin to steepen and break in water twice the depth of its height.

- Large swells hitting steep reefs, creates the biggest waves.
- Beach breaks tend to create more confused waves. A wave may peel along its whole length before dumping on the shore, as there is very little to slow the wave down.
- Point breaks or headlands concentrate the power of the swell into one area. This can create larger and more predictable waves.

Dumping waves & undertows

On steeply shelving beaches, especially at high tide, the force of incoming water suddenly reaching the shore causes waves to rise up and dump heavily on the shore. This is known as a 'shorebreak'. The power of the breaking waves against the shore can create sub-surface flow of water that moves inshore and then pulls seaward. A strong undertow can easily pull you out to sea.

Weather Effects

Sea breeze

If the land is hotter than the sea, warm air over the land rises and pulls the cooler air in from the sea, creating a sea breeze. This tends to happen in isolated areas along the coast during the summer when the difference between land and sea temperatures is at their greatest.

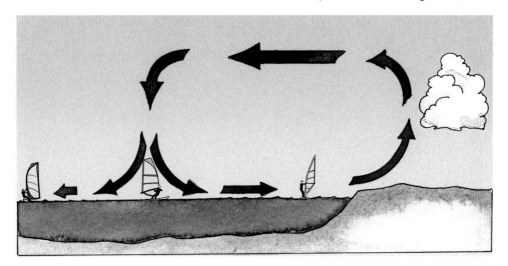

Weather maps & forecasts

News channels, internet sites and weather stations make it possible to obtain numerous forecasts and real time indications of conditions at windsurfing venues. Forecasts are not always accurate and it's worth being able to read the basics of a weather map to help make your own decision.

All you need to know can be found in the *RYA Weather Handbook* or *RYA Weather Forecasts*.

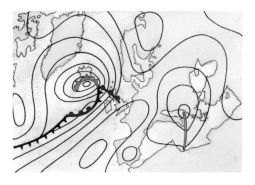

A high pressure, which is illustrated by well separated Isobars, indicates lighter winds. Local thermal effects and summer seabreezes mean you can still get good windsurfing wind in a high pressure area. However, widely spaced Isobars often indicate conditions best suited to a high volume board and light wind training.

A low pressure is indicated by converging tightly packed Isobars. This generally means strong winds are on their way.

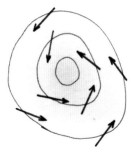

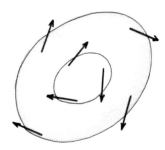

In a high pressure system the air moves clockwise and away from the centre. Early indications are reducing numbers of clouds due to the downwards and outwards flow of air, which usually creates clear skies.

In a low pressure system the air moves anti-clockwise towards the centre. Early indications are high Cirrus clouds, wind backing to the south and barometer begins to fall.

Buys Ballot's Law

- If you stand with your back to the wind (in the Northern Hemisphere) there will be a Low Pressure to your *left* and a High Pressure to your *right*.

Cumulus cloud after the cold front has passed

Cirrostratus and halo

Layers of cloud as the depression approaches

Warm & cold fronts

A Warm Front announces the arrival of a mass of *warm* air (stable air stream). Warm front indicators are thickening, lowering cloud, heavy persistent rain and a rise in temperature. Wind increases and backs, visibility diminishes in the rain and the barometer falls.

A Cold Front announces the arrival of a mass of *cold* air (unstable air stream). Early indications include Cumulus and often Cumulonimbus clouds, heavy showers, gusty winds veering to the north-west and a drop in temperature.

Warm Sector, between fronts, is typified by westerly winds and 'cumulus' clouds. Wind strength will be determined by closeness of Isobars.

Occluded Front, where the *warm* and *cold* fronts join, creates a mix of warm and cold air, often resulting in cold continuous rain.

Backing Wind, indicates the wind changes in an anti-clockwise direction, e.g. W to S.

Veering, wind changes in a clockwise direction, e.g. W to N.

Thermal winds

Some locations get 'reliable' thermal effects because the wind gets funnelled, squeezed or accelerated due to local geographical factors. This is usually due to a difference in temperature between the water and land, plus converging islands or mountains. A classic example of this is in Egypt where strong winds are generated down the Gulf of Suez and Gulf of Aqaba where the sea is sandwiched between large 'hot' land masses. The wind accelerates and intensifies where the land is hottest, which draws wind in towards the coastline.

Trade winds

Blowing in a north-east direction in the Northern Hemisphere and south-east in the Southern Hemisphere, Trade winds are the prevailing winds found in the tropics close to the equator. Windsurfers benefit from these 'trades' in areas like the Caribbean, where islands such as Margarita are renowned for consistent winds at specific times of year. Funneling effects between islands can increase the strength of the wind.

Scirocco

A southerly wind from the dry deserts of North Africa.

Tramontane

Northerly wind that blows between the Pyrenees and Massif Central down to the Mediterranean.

Levanter & Vendaval

Easterly and westerly winds that blow over south-west Spain and north-west Africa.

Mistral

A strong north-north-west wind that blows down the Rhone Valley and across the western Mediterranean.

Katabatic wind

From the Greek word Katabatikos meaning "going downhill". Katabatic winds occur due to high density air being pulled down a slope by gravity. A large scale version of a Katabatic wind is the cooling Mistral. A localized version of a Katabatic wind is created on summer afternoons at Vassiliki on the Greek island of Levkas where a fresh wind falls down a near vertical mountain and blows straight across the bay.

So What's Next?

We've given you the principal windsurfing skills and training exercises that will enable you to become an advanced windsurfer. From this point on, time on the water, focusing on key skills and accentuating your actions are fundamental to your progress. Whether you decide to become more adventurous and seek waves, fancy full on freestyle or just continue to enjoy your current level, Advanced Windsurfing contains all the contributing factors to take you as far as you want to go.

A Windsurfer's Glossary

Battens	Stiff, flexible rods providing strength and shape to sail
Beam reach	Direction approximately 90° away from the direction of the wind
Bearing away	Turning away from wind
Blasting	Moving quickly across the water
Broad reach	Direction approximately 135° away from the direction of the wind
Buys Ballot's Law	A way to determine positions of high and low pressure systems
Carve gybe	High wind planing gybe
Carving	Engaging the rails of the board to aid a turn or change in direction of the board
Clew	Rear (lower) corner of sail, which attaches to the end of the boom
Downhaul	Rope used to attach tack of the sail to the mastfoot, enabling rig tuning
Drop & Dig/Push stance	*See* Super 7
Duck gybe	Carve gybe achieved by 'ducking' the sail
Fastfwd Formula	National windsurfing coaching model (five principles of sailing – Vision, Trim, Balance, Power, Stance)
Fin	Curved foil attached to underside and tail of board providing directional stability
Freeride board	A board used for general recreational sailing and blasting
Freestyle board	Trick-orientated board
Freestyle Wave board	A manoeuvre-orientated board but maintaining high wind blasting performance
Groundswell	Swell in sea which has travelled a long distance
Gybing	A transition used to change direction downwind
Laydown gybe	Gybing tightly by 'laying' the rig lower on the water
Leech	Trailing edge of a sail
Leeward	Side of the board away from the wind
Luff	Leading edge of sail next to mast
Luffing	Altering course towards the wind
Outhaul	Rope used to attached the clew of the sail to the end of the boom

Overfalls	Inconsistencies and obstructions on seabed causing tidal flow to be uplifted
Planing	Where the board reaches sufficient speed to travel on the minimum of wetted area on the surface of the water
Pumping	Action of sheeting the sail in and scooping the mast forward to accelerate
Rails	Edges along side of board
Rig	Sail, mast and boom assembly
Rig Rotator	Specific movement of the rig in gybes
Rip currents	Currents that sweep along the shore and out to sea
Rocker lines	Describes variation in curvature of underside of board
Rule of Twelfths	Rule relating to variation in water flow as tide rises/falls
Sail 360°	Exercise to practise Rig Rotator
Sail quiver	A set of sails of varying size
Sea breeze	Thermal wind generated by temperature difference between land and sea
Sheeting in	Pulling boom in, back and down
Shifting & Switching	Specific footwork movement during a transition
Shore break	Waves breaking on beach
Spinning out	Board slides sideways when fin loses grip
Strap to strap gybe	Advanced variation of step gybe
Survival gybe	Gybe used in strong winds using an upwind approach
Tacking	Turn taking the nose of the board through the wind
Tail	Back of board
Thermal winds	An effect caused by winds funnelled, squeezed or accelerated due to local geographic conditions
Trade winds	Prevailing winds in tropics close to equator
Trim	Correctly balance board by adopting best body and rig position
Tuning	Adjustment of rig to find most effective set-up
UJ (Universal Joint)	Part of the mastfoot, allowing flexible movement of the rig
Uphauling	Raising the rig using the uphaul rope
Upwinders	Exercises simulating beginnings of tacks
Wave board	Board for high winds and rough water
Windswell	Wave formation and height caused by direction and strength of wind
Windward	Side of the board closer to the wind

Index

RYA MEMBERSHIP APPLICATION

IT'S ALL ABOUT YOU AND THE BOATING YOU DO

One of boating's biggest attractions is its freedom from rules and regulations. As an RYA member you'll play an active part in keeping it that way, as well as benefiting from free expert advice and information, plus discounts on a wide range of boating products, charts and publications.

To join the RYA, please complete the application form below and send it to The Membership Department, RYA, RYA House, Ensign Way, Hamble, Southampton, Hampshire SO31 4YA. You can also join online at www.rya.org.uk, or by phoning the membership department on +44 (0) 23 8060 4159. Whichever way you choose to apply, you can save money by paying by Direct Debit. A Direct Debit instruction is on the back of this form.

Be part of it

	Title	Forename	Surname	Gender	Date of Birth
Applicant ❶					D D / M M / Y Y Y Y
Applicant ❷					D D / M M / Y Y Y Y
Applicant ❸					D D / M M / Y Y Y Y
Applicant ❹					D D / M M / Y Y Y Y

E-mail Applicant ❶

E-mail Applicant ❷

E-mail Applicant ❸

E-mail Applicant ❹

Address

Post Code

Home Tel

Day Time Tel

Mobile Tel

Type of membership required (Tick Box)

Junior (0-11)   Annual rate £5 or **£5 if paying by Direct Debit**

Youth (12-17)   Annual rate £14 or **£11 if paying by Direct Debit**

Under 25   Annual rate £25 or **£22 if paying by Direct Debit**

Personal   Annual rate £43 or **£39 if paying by Direct Debit**

Family*   Annual rate £63 or **£59 if paying by Direct Debit**

Save money by completing the Direct Debit form overleaf

Please number up to three boating interests in order, with number one being your principal interest

Yacht Racing   Yacht Cruising   Dinghy Racing   Dinghy Cruising

Personal Watercraft   Sportboats & RIBs   Windsurfing   Motor Boating

Powerboat Racing   Canal Cruising   River Cruising

* *Family Membership: 2 adults plus any under 18s all living at the same address. Prices valid until 30/9/2011 One discount voucher is accepted for individual memberships, and two discount vouchers are accepted for family membership.*

IMPORTANT In order to provide you with membership benefits the details provided by you on this form and in the course of your membership will be maintained on a database. If you do not wish to receive information on member services and benefits please tick here ☐ By applying for membership of the RYA you agree to be bound by the RYA's standard terms and conditions (copies on request or at www.rya.org.uk)

Signature

Date   D D / M M / Y Y

Source Code

Joining Point Code

GET MORE FROM
YOUR BOATING
SUPPORT THE
RYA

RYA
Be part of it

PAY BY DIRECT DEBIT – AND SAVE MONEY

Instructions to your Bank or Building Society to pay by Direct Debit

Please fill in the form and send to:
Membership Department, Royal Yachting Association, RYA House, Ensign Way, Hamble, Southampton, Hampshire SO31 4YA.

DIRECT Debit

Name and full postal address of your Bank/Building Society

To the Manager | Bank/Building Society

Address

Postcode

Name(s) of Account Holder(s)

Branch Sort Code

Bank/Building Society Account Number

Originator's Identification Number

9	5	5	2	1	3

RYA Membership Number (For office use only)

Instructions to your Bank or Building Society

Please pay Royal Yachting Association Direct Debits from the account detailed in this instruction subject to the safeguards assured by The Direct Debit Guarantee. I understand that this instruction may remain with the Royal Yachting Association and, if so, details will be passed electronically to my Bank/Building Society.

Signature(s)

Date: /   /